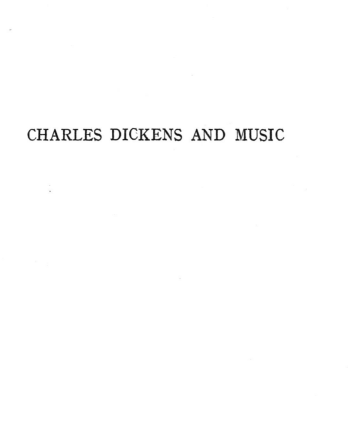

CHARLES DICKENS AND MUSIC

TOM PINCH AT THE ORGAN.

Frontispiece.

CHARLES DICKENS
AND MUSIC

BY

JAMES T. LIGHTWOOD

AUTHOR OF
' HYMN-TUNES AND THEIR STORY '

HASKELL HOUSE PUBLISHERS LTD.
Publishers of Scarce Scholarly Books
NEW YORK, N. Y. 10012
1970

First Published 1912

HASKELL HOUSE PUBLISHERS LTD.
Publishers of Scarce Scholarly Books
280 LAFAYETTE STREET
NEW YORK, N. Y. 10012

Library of Congress Catalog Card Number: **76-119084**

Standard Book Number 8383-1080-X

Printed in the United States of America

IN PLEASANT MEMORY

OF

MANY HAPPY YEARS

AT

PEMBROKE HOUSE, LYTHAM

PREFACE

FOR many years I have been interested in the various musical references in Dickens' works, and have had the impression that a careful examination of his writings would reveal an aspect of his character hitherto unknown, and, I may add, unsuspected. The centenary of his birth hastened a work long contemplated, and a first reading (after many years) brought to light an amount of material far in excess of what I anticipated, while a second examination convinced me that there is, perhaps, no great writer who has made a more extensive use of music to illustrate character and create incident than Charles Dickens. From an historical point of view these references are of the utmost importance, for they reflect to a nicety the general condition of ordinary musical life in England during the middle of the last century. We do not, of course, look to Dickens for a history of classical music during the period—those who want this will find it in the newspapers and magazines; but for the story of music in the ordinary English home, for the popular songs of the period, for the average musical attainments of the middle and lower classes (music was not the correct thing amongst the ' upper ten '), we must turn to the pages of Dickens' novels. It is certainly strange that no one has hitherto thought of tapping this source of information. In and about 1887 the papers teemed with articles that outlined the history of music during the first fifty years of Victoria's reign; but I have not seen one that attempted to derive first-hand information from the sources referred to, nor indeed does the subject of ' Dickens and Music ' ever appear to have received the attention which, in my opinion, it deserves.

I do not profess to have chronicled *all* the musical references, nor has it been possible to identify every one of the numerous quotations from songs, although I have consulted such excellent authorities as Dr. Cummings, Mr. Worden (Preston), and Mr. J. Allanson Benson (Bromley). I have to thank Mr. Frank Kidson, who, I understand, had already planned a work of this description, for his kind advice and assistance. There is no living writer who has such a wonderful knowledge of old songs as Mr. Kidson, a knowledge which he is ever ready to put at the disposal of others. Even now there are some half-dozen songs which every attempt to run to earth has failed, though I have tried to 'mole 'em out' (as Mr. Pancks would say) by searching through some hundreds of song-books and some thousands of separate songs.

Should any of my readers be able to throw light on dark places I shall be very glad to hear from them, with a view to making the information here presented as complete and correct as possible if another edition should be called for. May I suggest to the Secretaries of our Literary Societies, Guilds, and similar organizations that a pleasant evening might be spent in rendering some of the music referred to by Dickens. The proceedings might be varied by readings from his works or by historical notes on the music. Many of the pieces are still in print, and I shall be glad to render assistance in tracing them. Perhaps this idea will also commend itself to the members of the Dickens Fellowship, an organization with which all lovers of the great novelist ought to associate themselves.

JAMES T. LIGHTWOOD.

LYTHAM,
   October, 1912.

I truly love Dickens; and discern in the inner man of him a tone of real Music which struggles to express itself, as it may in these bewildered, stupefied and, indeed, very crusty and distracted days—better or worse!

THOMAS CARLYLE.

CONTENTS

LIST OF WORKS REFERRED TO

With Abbreviations Used

CHARLES DICKENS AND MUSIC

CHAPTER I

DICKENS AS A MUSICIAN

THE attempts to instil the elements of music into Charles Dickens when he was a small boy do not appear to have been attended with success. Mr. Kitton tells us that he learnt the piano during his school days, but his master gave him up in despair. Mr. Bowden, an old schoolfellow of the novelist's when he was at Wellington House Academy, in Hampstead Road, says that music used to be taught there, and that Dickens received lessons on the violin, but he made no progress, and soon relinquished it. It was not until many years after that he made his third and last attempt to become an instrumentalist. During his first transatlantic voyage he wrote to Forster telling him that he had bought an accordion.

The steward lent me one on the passage out, and I regaled the ladies' cabin with my performances. You can't think with what feelings I play ' Home, Sweet Home ' every night, or how pleasantly sad it makes us.

On the voyage back he gives the following description of the musical talents of his fellow
passengers :

> One played the accordion, another the violin, and another
> (who usually began at six o'clock a.m.) the key bugle : the
> combined effect of which instruments, when they all played
> different tunes, in different parts of the ship, at the same time,
> and within hearing of each other, as they sometimes did (every-
> body being intensely satisfied with his own performance), was
> sublimely hideous.

He does not tell us whether he was one of the
performers on these occasions.

But although he failed as an instrumentalist
he took delight in hearing music, and was always
an appreciative yet critical listener to what was good
and tuneful. His favourite composers were Mendelssohn—whose *Lieder* he was specially fond of[1]—
Chopin, and Mozart. He heard Gounod's *Faust* whilst
he was in Paris, and confesses to having been quite
overcome with the beauty of the music. ' I couldn't
bear it,' he says, in one of his letters, ' and gave in
completely. The composer must be a very remarkable man indeed.' At the same time he became
acquainted with Offenbach's music, and heard

---

[1] In his speech at Birmingham on ' Literature and Art ' (1853) he
makes special reference to the ' great music of Mendelssohn.'

Orphée aux enfers. This was in February, 1863. Here also he made the acquaintance of Auber, 'a stolid little elderly man, rather petulant in manner.' He told Dickens that he had lived for a time at 'Stock Noonton' (Stoke Newington) in order to study English, but he had forgotten it all. In the description of a dinner in the *Sketches* we read that

The knives and forks form a pleasing accompaniment to Auber's music, and Auber's music would form a pleasing accompaniment to the dinner, if you could hear anything besides the cymbals.

He met Meyerbeer on one occasion at Lord John Russell's. The musician congratulated him on his outspoken language on Sunday observance, a subject in which Dickens was deeply interested, and on which he advocated his views at length in the papers entitled *Sunday under Three Heads*.

Dickens was acquainted with Jenny Lind, and he gives the following amusing story in a letter to Douglas Jerrold, dated Paris, February 14, 1847 :

I am somehow reminded of a good story I heard the other night from a man who was a witness of it and an actor in it. At a certain German town last autumn there was a tremendous *furore* about Jenny Lind, who, after driving the whole place mad,

B

left it, on her travels, early one morning. The moment her
carriage was outside the gates, a party of rampant students
who had escorted it rushed back to the inn, demanded to be
shown to her bedroom, swept like a whirlwind upstairs into the
room indicated to them, tore up the sheets, and wore them in
strips as decorations. An hour or two afterwards a bald old
gentleman of amiable appearance, an Englishman, who was
staying in the hotel, came to breakfast at the *table d'hôte,* and
was observed to be much disturbed in his mind, and to show
great terror whenever a student came near him.   At last he
said, in a low voice, to some people who were near him at the
table, ' You are English gentlemen, I observe. Most extraordinary people, these Germans.   Students, as a body, raving
mad, gentlemen ! '   ' Oh, no,' said somebody else: ' excitable,
but very good fellows, and very sensible.' ' By God, sir ! '
returned the old gentleman, still more disturbed, ' then there's
something political in it, and I'm a marked man.   I went out for
a little walk this morning after shaving, and while I was gone '—
he fell into a terrible perspiration as he told it—' they burst
into my bedroom, tore up my sheets, and are now patrolling
the town in all directions with bits of 'em in their button-holes.'
I needn't wind up by adding that they had gone to the wrong
chamber.

It was Dickens' habit wherever he went on his
Continental travels to avail himself of any opportunity of visiting the opera ; and his criticisms,
though brief, are always to the point.   He tells
us this interesting fact about Carrara :

There is a beautiful little theatre there, built of marble, and
they had it illuminated that night in my honour.   There was

really a very fair opera, but it is curious that the chorus has been always, time out of mind, made up of labourers in the quarries, who don't know a note of music, and sing entirely by ear.

But much as he loved music, Dickens could never bear the least sound or noise while he was studying or writing, and he ever waged a fierce war against church bells and itinerant musicians. Even when in Scotland his troubles did not cease, for he writes about ' a most infernal piper practising under the window for a competition of pipers which is to come off shortly.' Elsewhere he says that he found Dover ' too bandy ' for him (he carefully explains he does not refer to its legs), while in a letter to Forster he complains bitterly of the vagrant musicians at Broadstairs, where he ' cannot write half an hour without the most excruciating organs, fiddles, bells, or glee singers.' The barrel-organ, which he somewhere calls an ' Italian box of music,' was one source of annoyance, but bells were his special aversion. ' If you know anybody at St. Paul's,' he wrote to Forster, ' I wish you'd send round and ask them not to ring the bell so. I can hardly hear my own ideas as they come into my head, and say what they mean.' His bell experiences at Genoa are referred to elsewhere (p. 57).

How marvellously observant he was is manifest

in the numerous references in his letters and works to the music he heard in the streets and squares of London and other places. Here is a description of Golden Square, London, W. (*N. N.*) :

Two or three violins and a wind instrument from the Opera band reside within its precincts. Its boarding-houses are musical, and the notes of pianos and harps float in the evening time round the head of the mournful statue, the guardian genius of the little wilderness of shrubs, in the centre of the square. . . . Sounds of gruff voices practising vocal music invade the evening's silence, and the fumes of choice tobacco scent the air. There, snuff and cigars and German pipes and flutes, and violins and violoncellos, divide the supremacy between them. It is the region of song and smoke. Street bands are on their mettle in Golden Square, and itinerant glee singers quaver involuntarily as they raise their voices within its boundaries.

We have another picture in the description of Dombey's house, where—

the summer sun was never on the street but in the morning, about breakfast-time. . . . It was soon gone again, to return no more that day, and the bands of music and the straggling Punch's shows going after it left it a prey to the most dismal of organs and white mice.

As a Singer

Most of the writers about Dickens, and especially his personal friends, bear testimony both to his vocal power and his love of songs and singing. As a small boy we read of him and his sister Fanny standing on a table singing songs, and acting them as they sang. One of his favourite recitations was Dr. Watts' ' The voice of the sluggard,' which he used to give with great effect. The memory of these words lingered long in his mind, and both Captain Cuttle and Mr. Pecksniff quote them with excellent appropriateness.

When he grew up he retained his love of vocal music, and showed a strong predilection for national airs and old songs. Moore's *Irish Melodies* had also a special attraction for him. In the early days of his readings his voice frequently used to fail him, and Mr. Kitton tells us that in trying to recover the lost power he would test it by singing these melodies to himself as he walked about. It is not surprising, therefore, to find numerous references to these songs, as well as to other works by Moore, in his writings.

From a humorous account of a concert on board ship we gather that Dickens possessed a tenor voice. Writing to his daughter from Boston in 1867, he says :

We had speech-making and singing in the saloon of the *Cuba* after the last dinner of the voyage. I think I have acquired a higher reputation from drawing out the captain, and getting him to take the second in ' All's Well ' and likewise in ' There's not in the wide world '¹ (your parent taking the first), than from anything previously known of me on these shores. . . . We also sang (with a Chicago lady, and a strong-minded woman from I don't know where) ' Auld Lang Syne,' with a tender melancholy expressive of having all four been united from our cradles. The more dismal we were, the more delighted the company were. Once (when we paddled i' the burn) the captain took a little cruise round the compass on his own account, touching at the Canadian Boat Song,² and taking in supplies at Jubilate, ' Seas between us braid ha' roared,' and roared like ourselves.

J. T. Field, in his *Yesterdays with Authors*, says : ' To hear him sing an old-time stage song, such as he used to enjoy in his youth at a cheap London theatre . . . was to become acquainted with one of the most delightful and original companions in the world.'

When at home he was fond of having music in the evening. His daughter tells us that on one occasion a member of his family was singing a song while he was apparently deep in his book, when he suddenly got up and saying ' You don't make enough of that word,' he sat down by the piano and showed how it should be sung.

On another occasion his criticism was more pointed.

¹ Moore's *Irish Melodies*.   ² Moore.

One night a gentleman visitor insisted on singing ' By the sad sea waves,' which he did vilely, and he wound up his performance by a most unexpected and misplaced embellishment, or ' turn.' Dickens found the whole ordeal very trying, but managed to preserve a decorous silence till this sound fell on his ear, when his neighbour said to him, ' Whatever did he mean by that extraneous effort of melody ? ' ' Oh,' said Dickens, ' that's quite in accordance with rule. When things are at their worst they always take a *turn*.'

Forster relates that while he was at work on the *Old Curiosity Shop* he used to discover specimens of old ballads in his country walks between Broadstairs and Ramsgate, which so aroused his interest that when he returned to town towards the end of 1840 he thoroughly explored the ballad literature of Seven Dials,[1] and would occasionally sing not a few of these wonderful discoveries with an effect that justified his reputation for comic singing in his childhood. We get a glimpse of his investigations in *Out of the Season*, where he tells us about that ' wonderful mystery, the music-shop,' with its assortment of polkas with coloured frontispieces, and also the book-shop, with its ' Little Warblers and Fairburn's Comic Songsters.'

[1] ' Seven Dials ! the region of song and poetry—first effusions and last dying speeches : hallowed by the names of Catnac and of Pitts, names that will entwine themselves with costermongers and barrel-organs, when penny magazines shall have superseded penny yards of song, and capital punishment be unknown ! ' (*S. B. S.* 5.)

Here too were ballads on the old ballad paper and in the old confusion of types, with an old man in a cocked hat, and an armchair, for the illustration to Will Watch the bold smuggler, and the Friar of Orders Grey, represented by a little girl in a hoop, with a ship in the distance.   All these as of yore, when they were infinite delights to me.

On one of his explorations he met a landsman who told him about the running down of an emigrant ship, and how he heard a sound coming over the sea ' like a great sorrowful flute or Aeolian harp.' He makes another and very humorous reference to this instrument in a letter to Landor, in which he calls to mind

that steady snore of yours, which I once heard piercing the door of your bedroom . . . reverberating along the bell-wire in the hall, so getting outside into the street, playing Aeolian harps among the area railings, and going down the New Road like the blast of a trumpet.

The deserted watering-place referred to in *Out of the Season* is Broadstairs, and he gives us a further insight into its musical resources in a letter to Miss Power written on July 2, 1847, in which he says that

a little tinkling box of music that stops at ' come ' in the melody of the Buffalo Gals, and can't play ' out to night,' and a white mouse, are the only amusements left at Broadstairs.

' Buffalo Gals ' was a very popular song ' Sung

with great applause by the Original Female American Serenaders.' (*c.* 1845.)   The first verse will explain the above allusion:

As I went lum'rin' down de street, down de street,
A 'ansom gal I chanc'd to meet, oh, she was fair to view.
Buffalo gals, can't ye come out to-night, come out to-night,
    come out to-night;
Buffalo gals, can't ye come out to-night, and dance by the light
    of the moon.

We find some interesting musical references and memories in the novelist's letters.   Writing to Wilkie Collins in reference to his proposed sea voyage, he quotes Campbell's lines from ' Ye Mariners of England ' :

As I sweep
Through the deep
When the stormy winds do blow.

There are other references to this song in the novels.   I have pointed out elsewhere that the last line also belongs to a seventeenth-century song.

Writing to Mark Lemon (June, 1849) he gives an amusing parody of

Lesbia hath a beaming eye,

beginning

Lemon is a little hipped.

In a letter to Maclise he says :

> My foot is in the house,
>   My bath is on the sea,
> And before I take a souse,
>   Here's a single note to thee.

These lines are a reminiscence of Byron's ode to Tom Moore, written from Venice on July 10, 1817 :

> My boat is on the shore,
>   And my bark is on the sea,
> But before I go, Tom Moore,
>   Here's a double health to thee !

The words were set to music by Bishop. This first verse had a special attraction for Dickens, and he gives us two or three variations of it, including a very apt one from Dick Swiveller (see p. 126).

Henry F. Chorley, the musical critic, was an intimate friend of Dickens. On one occasion he went to hear Chorley lecture on ' The National Music of the World,' and subsequently wrote him a very friendly letter criticizing his delivery, but speaking in high terms of the way he treated his subject.

In one of his letters he makes special reference

to the singing of the Hutchinson family.[1]   Writing
to the Countess of Blessington, he says :

> I must have some talk with you about these American singers.
> They must never go back to their own country without your
> having heard them sing Hood's ' Bridge of Sighs.'

Amongst the distinguished visitors at Gad's Hill
was Joachim, who was always a welcome guest, and
of whom Dickens once said ' he is a noble fellow.'
His daughter writes in reference to this visit :

> I never remember seeing him so wrapt and absorbed as he
> was then, on hearing him play ; and the wonderful simplicity and
> *un*-self-consciousness of the genius went straight to my father's
> heart, and made a fast bond of sympathy between those two
> great men.

In Music Drama

Much has been written about Dickens' undoubted
powers as an actor, as well as his ability as a stage
manager, and it is well known that it was little more

---

[1] The ' Hutchinson family' was a musical troupe composed of three
sons and two daughters selected from the ' Tribe of Jesse,' a name given
to the sixteen children of Jesse and Mary Hutchinson, of Milford, N.H.
They toured in England in 1845 and 1846, and were received with great
enthusiasm.   Their songs were on subjects connected with Temperance
and Anti-Slavery.   On one occasion Judson, one of the number, was
singing the ' Humbugged Husband,' which he used to accompany with
the fiddle, and he had just sung the line ' I'm sadly taken in,' when the
stage where he was standing gave way and he nearly disappeared from
view.   The audience at first took this as part of the performance.

than an accident that kept him from adopting the dramatic profession. He ever took a keen interest in all that pertained to the stage, and when he was superintending the production of a play he was always particular about the musical arrangements. There is in existence a play-bill of 1833 showing that he superintended a private performance of *Clari*. This was an opera by Bishop, and contains the first appearance of the celebrated ' Home, Sweet Home,' a melody which, as we have already said, he reproduced on the accordion some years after. He took the part of Rolano, but had no opportunity of showing off his singing abilities, unless he took a part in the famous glee ' Sleep, gentle lady,' which appears in the work as a quartet for alto, two tenors, and bass, though it is now arranged in other forms.

In his dealings with the drama Dickens was frequently his own bandmaster and director of the music. For instance, in *No Thoroughfare* we find this direction : ' Boys enter and sing " God Save the Queen " (or any school devotional hymn).' At Obenreizer's entrance a ' mysterious theme is directed to be played,' that gentleman being ' well informed, clever, and a good musician.'

Dickens was concerned in the production of one

operetta—*The Village Coquettes*—for which he wrote the words, and John Hullah composed the music. It consists of songs, duets, and concerted pieces, and was first produced at St. James's Theatre, London, on December 6, 1836. The following year it was being performed at Edinburgh when a fire broke out in the theatre, and the instrumental scores together with the music of the concerted pieces were destroyed. No fresh copy was ever made, but the songs are still to be obtained. Mr. Kitton, in his biography of the novelist, says, 'The play was well received, and duly praised by prominent musical journals.'

The same writer gives us to understand that Hullah originally composed the music for an opera called *The Gondolier*, but used the material for *The Village Coquettes*. Braham, the celebrated tenor, had a part in it. Dickens says in a letter to Hullah that he had had some conversation with Braham about the work. The singer thought very highly of it, and Dickens adds :

His only remaining suggestion is that Miss Rainforth [1] will want another song when the piece is in rehearsal—' a bravura— something in " The soldier tired " way.'

[1] Miss Rainforth was the soloist at the first production of Mendelssohn's ' Hear my Prayer.' (See *The Choir*, March, 1911.)

We have here a reference to a song which had a long run of popularity.   It is one of the airs in Arne's *Artaxerxes*, an opera which was produced in 1761, and which held the stage for many years.   There is a reference to this song in *Sketches by Boz*, when Miss Evans and her friends visited the Eagle.   During the concert ' Miss Somebody in white satin ' sang this air, much to the satisfaction of her audience.

Dickens wrote a few songs and ballads, and in most cases he fell in with the custom of his time, and suggested the tune (if any) to which they were to be sung.   In addition to those that appear in the various novels, there are others which deserve mention here.

In 1841 he contributed three political squibs in verse to the *Examiner*, one being the ' Quack Doctor's Proclamation,' to the tune of ' A Cobbler there was,' and another called ' The fine old English Gentleman.'

For the *Daily News* (of which he was the first editor) he wrote ' The British Lion, a new song but an old story,' which was to be sung to the tune of the ' Great Sea Snake.'   This was a very popular comic song of the period, which described a sea monster of wondrous size :

> One morning from his head we bore
>> With every stitch of sail,
> And going at ten knots an hour
>> In six months came to his tail.

Three of the songs in the *Pickwick Papers* (referred to elsewhere) are original, while Blandois' song in *Little Dorrit*, 'Who passes by this road so late,' is a translation from the French. This was set to music by R. S. Dalton.

In addition to these we find here and there impromptu lines which have no connexion with any song. Perhaps the best known are those which 'my lady Bowley' quotes in *The Chimes*, and which she had ' set to music on the new system ':

> Oh let us love our occupations,
> Bless the squire and his relations,
> Live upon our daily rations,
> And always know our proper stations.

The reference to the ' new system ' is not quite obvious. Dickens may have been thinking of the ' Wilhem ' method of teaching singing which his friend Hullah introduced into England, or it may be a reference to the Tonic Sol-fa system, which had already begun to make progress when *The Chimes* was written in 1844.[1]

[1] John Curwen published his *Grammar of Vocal Music* in 1842.

There are some well-known lines which owners of books were fond of writing on the fly-leaf in order that there might be no mistake as to the name of the possessor.   The general form was something like this :

> John Wigglesworth is my name,
>   And England is my nation ;
> London is my dwelling-place,
>   And Christ is my salvation.

(See *Choir*, Jan., 1912, p. 5.)   Dickens gives us at least two variants of this.   In *Edwin Drood*, Durdles says of the Mayor of Cloisterham :

> Mister Sapsea is his name,
>   England is his nation,
> Cloisterham's his dwelling-place,
>   Aukshneer's his occupation.

And Captain Cuttle thus describes himself, ascribing the authorship of the words to Job—but then literary accuracy was not the Captain's strong point :

> Cap'en Cuttle is my name,
>   And England is my nation,
> This here is my dwelling-place,
>   And blessed be creation.

It is said that there appeared in the *London*

Singer's Magazine for 1839 ' The Teetotal Excursion, an original Comic Song by Boz, sung at the London Concerts,' but it is not in my copy of this song-book, nor have I ever seen it.

Dickens was always very careful in his choice of names and titles, and the evolution of some of the latter is very interesting. One of the many he conceived for the magazine which was to succeed *Household Words* was *Household Harmony*, while another was *Home Music*. Considering his dislike of bells in general, it is rather surprising that two other suggestions were *English Bells* and *Weekly Bells*, but the final choice was *All the Year Round*. Only once does he make use of a musician's name in his novels, and that is in *Great Expectations*. Philip, otherwise known as Pip, the hero, becomes friendly with Herbert Pocket. The latter objects to the name Philip, ' it sounds like a moral boy out of a spelling-book,' and as Pip had been a blacksmith and the two youngsters were ' harmonious,' Pocket asks him :

' Would you mind Handel for a familiar name ? There's a charming piece of music, by Handel, called the " Harmonious Blacksmith." '

' I should like it very much.'

Dickens' only contribution to hymnology appeared

in the *Daily News* February 14, 1846, with the title
' Hymn of the Wiltshire Labourers.'   It was written
after reading a speech at one of the night meetings
of the wives of agricultural labourers in Wiltshire,
held with the object of petitioning for Free Trade.
This is the first verse :

O God, who by Thy Prophet's hand
  Did'st smite the rocky brake,
Whence water came at Thy command
  Thy people's thirst to slake,
Strike, now, upon this granite wall,
  Stern, obdurate, and high ;
And let some drop of pity fall
  For us who starve and die !

We find the fondness for Italian names shown by
vocalists and pianists humorously parodied in such
self-evident forms as Jacksonini, Signora Marra Boni,
and Billsmethi.   Banjo Bones is a self-evident *nom
d'occasion*, and the high-sounding name of Rinaldo di
Velasco ill befits the giant Pickleson (*Dr. M.*), who
had a little head and less in it.   As it was essential
that the Miss Crumptons of Minerva House should
have an Italian master for their pupils, we find
Signor Lobskini introduced, while the modern rage
for Russian musicians is to some extent anticipated
in Major Tpschoffki of the Imperial Bulgraderian

Brigade (*G. S.*).   His real name, if he ever had one, is said to have been Stakes.

Dickens has little to say about the music of his time, but in the reprinted paper called *Old Lamps for New Ones* (written in 1850), which is a strong condemnation of pre-Raphaelism in art, he attacks a similar movement in regard to music, and makes much fun of the Brotherhood. He detects their influence in things musical, and writes thus :

> In Music a retrogressive step, in which there is much hope, has been taken.   The P.A.B., or pre-Agincourt Brotherhood, has arisen, nobly devoted to consign to oblivion Mozart, Beethoven, Handel, and every other such ridiculous reputation, and to fix its Millennium (as its name implies) before the date of the first regular musical composition known to have been achieved in England.   As this institution has not yet commenced active operations, it remains to be seen whether the Royal Academy of Music will be a worthy sister of the Royal Academy of Art, and admit this enterprising body to its orchestra.   We have it, on the best authority, that its compositions will be quite as rough and discordant as the real old original.

Fourteen years later he makes use of a well-known phrase in writing to his friend Wills (October 8, 1864) in reference to the proofs of an article.

> I have gone through the number carefully, and have been down upon Chorley's paper in particular, which was a ' little

bit ' too personal.   It is all right now and good, and them's my
sentiments too of the Music of the Future.[1]

Although there was little movement in this
direction when Dickens wrote this, the paragraph
makes interesting reading nowadays in view of
some musical tendencies in certain quarters.

[1] Quoted in Mr. R. C. Lehmann's *Dickens as an Editor* (1912).

CHAPTER II

INSTRUMENTAL COMBINATIONS

VIOLIN, VIOLONCELLO, HARP, PIANO

DICKENS' orchestras are limited, both in resources and in the number of performers ; in fact, it would be more correct to call them combinations of instruments. Some of them are of a kind not found in modern works on instrumentation, as, for instance, at the party at Trotty Veck's (*Ch.*) when a 'band of music' burst into the good man's room, consisting of a drum, marrow-bones and cleavers, and bells, 'not *the* bells but a portable collection on a frame.' We gather from Leech's picture that other instrumentalists were also present. Sad to relate, the drummer was not quite sober, an unfortunate state of things, certainly, but not always confined to the drumming fraternity, since in the account of the Party at Minerva House (*S. B. T.*) we read that amongst the numerous arrivals were 'the pianoforte player and the violins : the harp in a state of intoxication.'

We have an occasional mention of a theatre orchestra, as, for instance, when the Phenomenon was performing at Portsmouth (*N. N.*) :

' Ring in the orchestra, Grudden.'

That useful lady did as she was requested, and shortly afterwards the tuning of three fiddles was heard, which process, having been protracted as long as it was supposed that the patience of the orchestra could possibly bear it, was put a stop to by another jerk of the bell, which, being the signal to begin in earnest, set the orchestra playing a variety of popular airs with involuntary variations.

On one occasion Dickens visited Vauxhall Gardens by day, where ' a small party of dismal men in cocked hats were "executing" the overture to *Tancredi*,' but he does not, unfortunately, give us any details about the number or kind of instruments employed. This would be in 1836, when the experiment of day entertainments was given a trial, and a series of balloon ascents became the principal attraction. Forster tells us that Dickens was a frequent visitor at the numerous gardens and places of entertainment which abounded in London, and which he knew better than any other man. References will be found elsewhere to the music at the Eagle (p. 47) and the White Conduit Gardens (p. 93).

Violin and Kit.

We meet with but few players on the violin, and it is usually mentioned in connexion with other instruments, though it was to the strains of a solitary fiddle that Simon Tappertit danced a hornpipe for the delectation of his followers, while the same instrument supplied the music at the Fezziwig's ball.

In came a fiddler with a music-book, and went up to the lofty desk, and made an orchestra of it, and tuned liked fifty stomach-aches.

The orchestra at the ' singing-house ' provided for Jack's amusement when ashore (*U. T.* 5) consisted of a fiddle and tambourine ; while at dances the instruments were fiddles and harps. It was the harps that first aroused Mr. Jingle's curiosity, as he met them being carried up the staircase of The Bull at Rochester, while, shortly after, the tuning of both harps and fiddles inspired Mr. Tupman with a strong desire to go to the ball. Sometimes the orchestra is a little more varied. At the private theatricals which took place at Mrs. Gattleton's (*S. B. T.* 9), the selected instruments were a piano, flute, and violoncello, but there seems to have been a want of proper rehearsal.

Ting, ting, ting ! went the prompter's bell at eight o'clock precisely, and dash went the orchestra into the overture to the *Men of Prometheus.* The pianoforte player hammered away with laudable perseverance, and the violoncello, which struck in at intervals, sounded very well, considering. The unfortunate individual, however, who had undertaken to play the flute accompaniment ' at sight' found, from fatal experience, the perfect truth of the old adage, ' Out of sight, out of mind '; for being very near-sighted, and being placed at a considerable distance from his music-book, all he had an opportunity of doing was to play a bar now and then in the wrong place, and put the other performers out. It is, however, but justice to Mr. Brown to say that he did this to admiration. The overture, in fact, was not unlike a race between the different instruments ; the piano came in first by several bars, and the violoncello next, quite distancing the poor flute ; for the deaf gentleman *too-too'd* away, quite unconscious that he was at all wrong, until apprised, by the applause of the audience, that the overture was concluded.

It was probably after this that the pianoforte player fainted away, owing to the heat, and left the music of *Masaniello* to the other two. There were differences between these remaining musicians and Mr. Harleigh, who played the title rôle, the orchestra complaining that ' Mr. Harleigh put them out, while the hero declared that the orchestra prevented his singing a note.'

It was to the strains of a wandering harp and fiddle that Marion and Grace Jeddler danced ' a trifle in the Spanish style,' much to their father's astonishment as he came bustling out to see who ' played music on his property before breakfast.'

The little fiddle commonly known as a ' kit ' that dancing-masters used to carry in their capacious tail coat pockets was much more in evidence in the middle of last century than it is now. Cadby Jellyby (*B. H.*), after her marriage to a dancing-master, found a knowledge of the piano and the kit essential, and so she used to practise them assiduously. When Sampson Brass hears Kit's name for the first time he says to Swiveller :

' Strange name—name of a dancing-master's fiddle, eh, Mr. Richard ? '

We must not forget the story of a fine young Irish gentleman, as told by the one-eyed bagman to Mr. Pickwick and his friends, who,

being asked if he could play the fiddle, replied he had no doubt he could, but he couldn't exactly say for certain, because he had never tried.

Violoncello

Mr. Morfin (*D. & S.*), ' a cheerful-looking, hazel-eyed elderly bachelor,' was

a great musical amateur—in his way—after business, and had a paternal affection for his violoncello, which was once in every week transported from Islington, his place of abode, to a certain club-room hard by the Bank, where quartets of the most tormenting and excruciating nature were executed every Wednesday evening by a private party.

His habit of humming his musical recollections of these evenings was a source of great annoyance to Mr. James Carker, who devoutly wished ' that he would make a bonfire of his violoncello, and burn his books with it.'   There was only a thin partition between the rooms which these two gentlemen occupied, and on another occasion Mr. Morfin performed an extraordinary feat in order to warn the manager of his presence.

I have whistled, hummed tunes, gone accurately through the whole of Beethoven's Sonata in B, to let him know that I was within hearing, but he never heeded me.

This particular sonata has not hitherto been identified.

It is comforting to know that the fall of the House of Dombey made no difference to Mr. Morfin, who continued to solace himself by producing ' the most dismal and forlorn sounds out of his violoncello before going to bed,' a proceeding which had no effect on his deaf landlady, beyond producing ' a sensation of something rumbling in her bones.'

Nor were the quartet parties interfered with. They came round regularly, his violoncello was in good tune, and there was nothing wrong in *his* world.   Happy Mr. Morfin !

Another 'cellist was the Rev. Charles Timson, who, when practising his instrument in his bedroom, used to give strict orders that he was on no account to be disturbed.

It was under the pretence of buying ' a second-hand wiolinceller ' that Bucket visited the house of the dealer in musical instruments in order to effect the arrest of Mr. George (*B. H.*).

Harp

The harp was a fashionable drawing-room instrument in the early Victorian period, although the re-introduction of the guitar temporarily detracted from its glory.   It was also indispensable in providing music for dancing-parties and concerts. When Esther Summerson went to call on the Turveydrops (*B. H.*) she found the hall blocked up with a grand piano, a harp, and various other instruments which had been used at a concert.   As already stated, it was the sight of these instruments being carried up the stairs at The Bull in Rochester that aroused Mr. Jingle's curiosity (*P. P.*) and led to the discovery that a ball was in prospect.

We must not forget the eldest Miss Larkins, one of David Copperfield's early, fleeting loves. He used to wander up and down outside the home of his beloved and watch the officers going in to hear Miss L. play the harp. On hearing of her engagement to one of these he mourned for a very brief period, and then went forth and gloriously defeated his old enemy the butcher boy. What a contrast between this humour and the strange scene in the drawing-room at James Steerforth's home after Rosa Dartle had sung the strange weird Irish song to the accompaniment of her harp ! And how different, again, the scene in the home of Scrooge's nephew (*C. C.*) when, after tea, ' they had some music.'

Scrooge's niece played well upon the harp ; and played, among other things, a simple little air.

It reminded Scrooge of a time long past.

He softened more and more ; and thought that if he could have listened to it often, years ago, he might have cultivated the kindnesses of life for his own happiness with his own hand.

Little Paul Dombey told Lady Skettles at the breaking-up party that he was very fond of music, and he was very, very proud of his sister's accomplishments both as player and singer. Did they inherit this love from their father ? ' You are fond of music,' said the Hon. Mrs. Skewton to Mr. Dombey during an interval in a game of picquet. ' Eminently so,' was the reply. But the reader must not take him at his word. When Edith (the future Mrs. Dombey) entered the room and sat down to her harp,

Mr. Dombey rose and stood beside her, listening. He had little taste for music, and no knowledge of the strain she played ; but he saw her bending over it, and perhaps he heard among the sounding strings some distant music of his own.

Yet when she went to the piano and commenced to sing Mr. Dombey did not know that it was ' the air that his neglected daughter sang to his dead son ' !

Piano

Lady musicians are numerous, and of very varied degrees of excellence. Amongst the pianists is Miss Teresa Malderton, who nearly fell a prey to that gay deceiver Mr. Horatio Sparkins (*S. B. T.* 5). Her contribution to a musical evening was ' The Fall of Paris,' played, as Mr. Sparkins declared, in a masterly manner.

There was a song called ' The Fall of Paris,' but
it is most probable that Dickens was thinking of a
very popular piece which he must have often heard
in his young days, of which the full title was

THE SURRENDER OF PARIS. A characteristic Divertimento
for the Pianoforte, including the events from the Duke of Wellington and Prince Blucher's marching to that capital to the
evacuation by the French troops and taking possession by the
Allies, composed by Louis Jansen, 1816.

Not the least curious section of this piece of early
programme music is a *moderato* recording the various
articles of the capitulation.   These are eighteen in
number, and each has its own ' theme.'   The inter-
spersion of some discords seems to imply serious
differences of opinion between the parties to the
treaty.

There was also a song called ' The Downfall of
Paris,' the first verse of which was

> Great news I have to tell you all,
>   Of Bonaparte and a' that ;
> How Paris it has got a fall,
>   He's lost his plans and a' that.
>
>   *Chorus.*
> Rise up, John Bull, rise up and sing,
>   Your chanter loudly blaw that ;
> Lang live our auld and worthy king,
>   Success to Britain, a' that.

The instrument beloved of Miss Tox (*D. & S.*) was the harpsichord, and her favourite piece was the ' Bird Waltz,' while the ' Copenhagen Waltz ' was also in her repertoire. Two notes of the instrument were dumb from disuse, but their silence did not impoverish the rendering. Cadby Jellyby found it necessary to know something of the piano, in order that she might instruct the ' apprentices ' at her husband's dancing-school. Another performer was Mrs. Namby, who entertained Mr. Pickwick with solos on a square piano while breakfast was being prepared. When questioned by David Copperfield as to the gifts of Miss Sophy Crewler, Traddles explained that she knew enough of the piano to teach it to her little sisters, and she also sang ballads to freshen up her family a little when they were out of spirits, but ' nothing scientific.' The guitar was quite beyond her. David noted with much satisfaction (though he did not say so) that his Dora was much more gifted musically.

When Dickens wrote his earlier works it was not considered the correct thing for a gentleman to play the piano, though it might be all very well for the lower classes and the music teacher. Consequently we read of few male performers on the instrument. Mr. Skimpole could play the piano, and of course Jasper had a ' grand ' in his room at Cloisterham.

At one time, if we may believe the turnkey at the Marshalsea prison, William Dorrit had been a pianist, a fact which raised him greatly in the turnkey's opinion.

> Brought up as a gentleman, he was, if ever a man was. Educated at no end of expense. Went into the Marshal's house once to try a new piano for him. Played it, I understand, like one o'clock—beautiful.

In the *Collected Papers* we have a picture of the ' throwing off young gentleman,' who strikes a note or two upon the piano, and accompanies it correctly (by dint of laborious practice) with his voice. He assures

> a circle of wondering listeners that so acute was his ear that he was wholly unable to sing out of tune, let him try as he would.

Mr. Weller senior laid a deep plot in which a piano was to take a prominent part. His object was to effect Mr. Pickwick's escape from the Fleet.

> Me and a cab'net-maker has dewised a plan for gettin' him out. ' A pianner, Samivel, a pianner,' said Mr. Weller, striking his son on the chest with the back of his hand, and falling back a step or two.
>
> ' Wot do you mean ? ' said Sam.
>
> ' A pianner-forty, Samivel,' rejoined Mr. Weller, in a still

more mysterious manner, ' as he can have on hire ; vun as von't play, Sammy.'

' And wot 'ud be the good of that ? ' said Sam.

' There ain't no vurks in it,' whispered his father. ' It 'ull hold him easy, vith his hat and shoes on ; and breathe through the legs, vich is holler.'

But the usually dutiful Sam showed so little enthusiasm for his father's scheme that nothing more was heard of it.

CHAPTER III

VARIOUS INSTRUMENTS
FLUTE, ORGAN, GUITAR (AND SOME HUMMERS)

Flute

WE find several references to the flute, and Dickens contrives to get much innocent fun out of it. First comes Mr. Mell, who used to carry his instrument about with him and who, in response to his mother's invitation to ' have a blow at it ' while David Copperfield was having his breakfast, made, said David, ' the most dismal sounds I have ever heard produced by any means, natural or artificial.' After he had finished he unscrewed his flute into three pieces, and deposited them underneath the skirts of his coat.

Dickens' schoolmasters seem to have been partial to the flute. Mr. Squeers, it is true, was not a flautist, but Mr. Feeder, B.A., was, or rather he was going to be. When little Paul Dombey visited his tutor's room he saw ' a flute which Mr. Feeder couldn't play yet, but was going to make a point of learning, he said, hanging up over the fireplace.'

He also had a beautiful little curly second-hand 'key bugle,' which was also on the list of things to be accomplished on some future occasion, in fact he has unlimited confidence in the power and influence of music. Here is his advice to the love-stricken Mr. Toots, whom he recommends to

learn the guitar, or at least the flute ; for women like music when you are paying your addresses to 'em, and he has found the advantage of it himself.

The flute was the instrument that Mr. Richard Swiveller took to when he heard that Sophy Wackles was lost to him for ever,

thinking that it was a good, sound, dismal occupation, not only in unison with his own sad thoughts, but calculated to awaken a fellow feeling in the bosoms of his neighbours.

So he got out his flute, arranged the light and a small oblong music-book to the best advantage, and began to play ' most mournfully.'

The air was ' Away with Melancholy,' a composition which, when it is played very slowly on the flute, in bed, with the further disadvantage of being performed by a gentleman but imperfectly acquainted with the instrument, who repeats one note a great many times before he can find the next, has not a lively effect.

So Mr. Swiveller spent half the night or more over this pleasing exercise, merely stopping now and then to take breath and soliloquize about the Marchioness; and it was only after he ' had nearly maddened the people of the house, and at both the next doors, and over the way,' that he shut up the book and went to sleep. The result of this was that the next morning he got a notice to quit from his landlady, who had been in waiting on the stairs for that purpose since the dawn of day.

Jack Redburn, too (*M. H. C.*), seems to have found consolation in this instrument, spending his wet Sundays in ' blowing a very slow tune on the flute.'

There is one, and only one, recorded instance of this very meek instrument suddenly asserting itself by going on strike, and that is in the sketch entitled *Private Theatres* (*S. B. S.* 13), where the amateurs take so long to dress for their parts that ' the flute says he'll be blowed if he plays any more.'

We must on no account forget the serenade with which the gentlemen boarders proposed to honour the Miss Pecksniffs. The performance was both vocal and instrumental, and the description of the flute-player is delightful.

It was very affecting, very. Nothing more dismal could have been desired by the most fastidious taste. . . . The youngest gentleman blew his melancholy into a flute. He didn't blow much out of it, but that was all the better.

After a description of the singing we have more about the flute.

> The flute of the youngest gentleman was wild and fitful. It came and went in gusts, like the wind. For a long time together he seemed to have left off, and when it was quite settled by Mrs. Todgers and the young ladies that, overcome by his feelings, he had retired in tears, he unexpectedly turned up again at the very top of the tune, gasping for breath. He was a tremendous performer. There was no knowing where to have him ; and exactly when you thought he was doing nothing at all, then was he doing the very thing that ought to astonish you most.

Yet another performer is the domestic young gentleman (*C. P.*) who holds skeins of silk for the ladies to wind, and who then

> brings down his flute in compliance with a request from the youngest Miss Gray, and plays divers tunes out of a very small book till supper-time.

When Nancy went to the prison to look for Oliver Twist, she found nobody in durance vile except a man who had been taken up for playing the flute, and who was bewailing the loss of the same, which had been confiscated for the use of the county.

The gentleman who played the violoncello at Mrs. Gattleton's party has already been referred to, and it only remains to mention Mr. Evans, who 'had such lovely whiskers ' and who played the flute on the same occasion, to bring the list of players to an end.

Hummers

We meet with a remarkable musician in *Dombey and Son* in the person of Harriet Carker's visitor, a scientific one, according to the description :

> A certain skilful action of his fingers as he hummed some bars, and beat time on the seat beside him, seemed to denote the musician ; and the extraordinary satisfaction he derived from humming something very slow and long, which had no recognizable time, seemed to denote that he was a scientific one.

A less capable performer was Sampson Brass, who hummed

> in a voice that was anything but musical certain vocal snatches which appeared to have reference to the union between Church and State, inasmuch as they were compounded of the Evening Hymn and ' God Save the King.'

Musicians of various degrees abound in the *Sketches*. Here is Mr. Wisbottle, whistling ' The Light Guitar ' at five o'clock in the morning, to the intense disgust of Mr. John Evenson, a fellow boarder at Mrs. Tibbs'. Subsequently he came down to breakfast in blue slippers and a shawl dressing-gown, whistling ' Di piacer.' Mr. Evenson can no longer control his feelings, and threatens to start the triangle if his enemy will not stop his early matutinal music. A suggested name for this whistler is the 'humming-top,' from his habit of describing semi-circles on the piano stool, and 'humming most melodiously.' There are a number of characters who indulge in the humming habit either to cover their confusion, or as a sign of light-heartedness and contentment. Prominent amongst these are Pecksniff, who, like Morfin, hums melodiously, and Micawber, who can both sing and hum. Nor must we omit to mention Miss Petowker, who ' hummed a tune ' as her contribution to the entertainment at Mrs. Kenwigs' party. Many of the characters resort to humming to conceal their temporary discomfiture, and perhaps no one ever hummed under more harassing circumstances than when Mr. Pecksniff had to go to the door to let in some very unwelcome guests, who had already knocked several times. But he was a past master in the art of dissimulation. He is particularly anxious to conceal from his visitors the fact that Jonas Chuzzlewit is in the house. So he says to the latter—

' This may be a professional call. Indeed I am pretty sure it is. Thank you.' Then Mr. Pecksniff, gently warbling a rustic stave, put on his garden hat, seized a spade, and opened the street door ; calmly appearing on the threshold as if he thought he had, from his vineyard, heard a modest rap, but was not quite certain.

Then he tells his visitors ' I do a little bit of Adam still.' He certainly had a good deal of the old Adam in him.

Clarionet

The clarionet is associated with the fortunes of Mr. Frederick Dorrit, who played the instrument at the theatre where his elder niece was a dancer, and where Little Dorrit sought an engagement. After the rehearsal was over she and her sister went to take him home.

He had been in that place six nights a week for many years, but had never been observed to raise his eyes above his music-book. . . . The carpenters had a joke that he was dead without being aware of it.

At the theatre he had no part in what was going on except the part written for the clarionet. In his young days his house had been the resort of singers and players. When the fortunes of the family changed his clarionet was taken away from him, on the ground that it was a ' low instrument.' It was subsequently restored to him, but he never played it again.

Of quite a different stamp was one of the characters in *Going into Society*, who played the clarionet in a band at a Wild Beast Show, and played it all wrong. He was somewhat eccentric in dress, as he had on ' a white Roman shirt and a bishop's mitre covered with leopard skin.' We are told nothing about him, except that he refused to know his old friends. In his story of the *Seven Poor Travellers* Dickens found the clarionet-player of the Rochester Waits so communicative that he accompanied the party across an open green called the Vines,

and assisted—in the French sense—at the performance of two waltzes, two polkas, and three Irish melodies.

Bassoon

A notable bassoon player was Mr. Bagnet, who had a voice somewhat resembling his instrument. The ex-artilleryman kept a little music shop in a street near the Elephant and Castle. There were

a few fiddles in the window, and some Pan's pipes and a tambourine, and a triangle, and certain elongated scraps of music.

It was to this shop that Bucket the detective came under the pretence of wanting a second-hand

' wiolinceller ' (see p. 29). In the course of conversation it turns out that Master Bagnet (otherwise ' Woolwich ') ' plays the fife beautiful,' and he performs some popular airs for the benefit of his audience. Mr. Bucket also claims to have played the fife himself when a boy, ' not in a scientific way, but by ear.'

Bagpipes

Two references to the bagpipes deserve notice. One is in *David Copperfield*, where the novelist refers to his own early experiences as a shorthand reporter. He has no high opinion of the speeches he used to take down.

One joyful night, therefore, I noted down the music of the parliamentary bagpipes for the last time, and I have never heard it since ; though I still recognize the old drone in the newspapers.

In *O. M. F.* (II.) we read of Charley Hexam's fellow pupils keeping themselves awake

by maintaining a monotonous droning noise, as if they were performing, out of time and tune, on a ruder sort of bagpipe.

The peculiar subdued noise caused by a lot of children in a school is certainly suggestive of the instrument.

Trombone

Little is said about the trombone. We are told, in reference to the party at Dr. Strong's (*D. C.*), that the good Doctor knew as much about playing cards as he did about ' playing the trombone.' In ' Our School' (*R. P.*) we are told a good deal about the usher who ' made out the bills, mended the pens, and did all sorts of things.'

He was rather musical, and on some remote quarter-day had bought an old trombone ; but a bit of it was lost, and it made the most extraordinary sounds when he sometimes tried to play it of an evening.

In a similarly dismembered state was the flute which Dickens once saw in a broker's shop. It was ' complete with the exception of the middle joint.'

This naturally calls to mind the story of the choir librarian who was putting away the vocal parts of a certain funeral anthem. After searching in vain for two missing numbers he was obliged to label the parcel

' His body is buried in peace.'   Two parts missing.

Organ

The references to the organ are both numerous and interesting, and it is pretty evident that this

instrument had a great attraction for Dickens.   The
gentle Tom Pinch (*M. C.*), whom Gissing calls 'a
gentleman who derives his patent of gentility direct
from God Almighty,' first claims our attention.   He
used to play the organ at the village church ' for
nothing.'   It was a simple instrument, 'the sweetest
little organ you ever heard,' provided with wind
by the action of the musician's feet, and thus Tom
was independent of a blower, though he was so
beloved that

> there was not a man or boy in all the village and away to the
> turnpike (tollman included) but would have blown away for him
> till he was black in the face.

What a delight it must have been to him to avail
himself of the opportunity to play the organ in the
cathedral when he went to meet Martin !

> As the grand tones resounded through the church they seemed,
> to Tom, to find an echo in the depth of every ancient tomb,
> no less than in the deep mystery of his own heart.

And he would have gone on playing till midnight
' but for a very earthy verger,' who insisted on locking
up the cathedral and turning him out.

On one occasion, while he was practising at the
church, the miserable Pecksniff entered the building
and, hiding behind a pew, heard the conversation

between Tom and Mary that led to the former being dismissed from the architect's office, so he had to leave his beloved organ, and mightily did the poor fellow miss it when he went to London ! Being an early riser, he had been accustomed to practise every morning, and now he was reduced to taking long walks about London, a poor substitute indeed !

Nor was the organ the only instrument that he could play, for we read how he would spend half his nights poring over the ' jingling anatomy of that inscrutable old harpsichord in the back parlour,' and amongst the household treasures that he took to London were his music and an old fiddle.

The picture which forms our frontispiece shows Tom Pinch playing his favourite instrument. At the sale of the original drawings executed by ' Phiz ' for *Martin Chuzzlewit* this frontispiece, which is an epitome of the salient characters and scenes in the novel, was sold for £35.

We read in *Christmas Stories* that

> Silas Jorgan
> Played the organ,

but we are not told the name of the artist who at the concert at the Eagle (*S. B. C.* 4) accompanied a comic song on the organ—and such an organ !

Miss J'mima Ivins's friend's young man whispered it had cost ' four hundred pound,' which Mr. Samuel Wilkins said was ' not dear neither.'

The singer was probably either Howell or Glindon. Dickens appears to have visited the Eagle Tavern in 1835 or 1836. It was then a notable place of entertainment consisting of gardens with an orchestra, and the ' Grecian Saloon,' which was furnished with an organ and a ' self-acting piano.' Here concerts were given every evening, which in Lent took a sacred turn, and consisted of selections from Handel and Mozart. In 1837 the organ was removed, and a new one erected by Parsons.

The Eagle gained a wide reputation through its being introduced into a once popular song.

> Up and down the City Road,
> In and out the Eagle,
> That's the way the money goes,
> Pop goes the weasel.

This verse was subsequently modified (for nursery purposes) thus :

> Half a pound of tuppenny rice,
> Half a pound of treacle,
> That's the way the money goes,[1]
> Pop goes the weasel.

[1] Or, ' Mix it up and make it nice.'

Many explanations have been given of ' weasel.'
Some say it was a purse made of weasel skin ; others
that it was a tailor's flat-iron which used to be
pawned (or ' popped ') to procure the needful for
admission to the tavern. A third (and more intelli-
gible) suggestion is that the line is simply a catch
phrase, without any meaning.

There is a notable reference to the organ in *Little
Dorrit*. Arthur Clennam goes to call on old
Frederick Dorrit, the clarionet player, and is
directed to the house where he lived. ' There were
so many lodgers in this house that the door - post
seemed to be as full of bell handles as a cathedral
organ is of stops,' and Clennam hesitates for a time,
' doubtful which might be the clarionet stop.'

Further on in the same novel we are told that
it was the organ that Mrs. Finching was desirous
of learning.

I have said ever since I began to recover the blow of Mr. F's
death that I would learn the organ of which I am extremely
fond but of which I am ashamed to say I do not yet know a note.

The following fine description of the tones of an
organ occurs in *The Chimes* :

The organ sounded faintly in the church below. Swelling
by degrees the melody ascended to the roof, and filled the choir

and nave. Expanding more and more, it rose up, up ; up, up ; higher, higher, higher up ; awakening agitated hearts within the burly piles of oak, the hollow bells, the iron-bound doors, the stairs of solid stone ; until the tower walls were insufficient to contain it, and it soared into the sky.

The effect of this on Trotty Veck was very different from that which another organ had on the benevolent old lady we read of in *Our Parish*. She subscribed £20 towards a new instrument for the parish church, and was so overcome when she first heard it that she had to be carried out by the pew-opener.

There are various references to the organs in the City churches, and probably the description of one of them given in *Dombey and Son* would suit most instruments of the period.

The organ rumbled and rolled as if it had got the colic, for want of a congregation to keep the wind and damp out.

Barrel-Organ

In real life the barrel-organ was a frequent source of annoyance to Dickens, who found its ceaseless strains very trying when he was busy writing. and who had as much trouble in evicting the grinders as David Copperfield's aunt had with the donkeys.

However, he takes a very mild revenge on this deservedly maligned instrument in his works, and the references are, as usual, of a humorous character. A barrel-organ formed a part of the procession to celebrate the election of Mr. Tulrumble[1] as Mayor of Mudfog, but the player put on the wrong stop, and played one tune while the band played another.

This instrument had an extraordinary effect on Major Tpschoffki, familiarly and more easily known as ' Chops,' the dwarf, 'spirited but not proud,' who was desirous of ' Going into Society ' (*G. S.*), and who had got it into his head that he was entitled to property :

His ideas respectin' his property never come upon him so strong as when he sat upon a barrel-organ, and had the handle turned. Arter the wibration had run through him a little time he would screech out, ' Toby, I feel my property coming—grind away ! I'm counting my guineas by thousands, Toby—grind away ! Toby, I shall be a man of fortun ! I feel the Mint a-jingling in me, Toby, and I'm swelling out into the Bank of England.' Such is the influence of music on a poetic mind.

Dickens found the streets in New York very different from those in London, and specially remarks how quiet they were—no itinerant musicians

[1] *The Public Life of Mr. Tulrumble*, 1837.

E

or showmen of any kind.   He could only remember
hearing one barrel-organ with a dancing-monkey.
' Beyond that, nothing lively, no, not so much as a
white mouse in a twirling cage.'

We must not forget that he has two references to
pipe organs in his *American Notes*. When he visited
the Blind School at Boston he heard a voluntary
played on the organ by one of the pupils, while
at St. Louis he was informed that the Jesuit
College was to be supplied with an organ sent from
Belgium.

The barrel-organ brings to mind Jerry and his
troupe of dancing-dogs (*O. C. S.*), especially the
unfortunate animal who had lost a halfpenny during
the day, and consequently had to go without his
supper.   In fact, his master made the punishment
fit the crime ;   for, having set the stop, he made the
dog play the organ while the rest had their evening
meal.

When the knives and forks rattled very much, or any of his
fellows got an unusually large piece of fat, he accompanied the
music with a short howl ; but he immediately checked it on his
master looking round, and applied himself with increased diligence
to the Old Hundredth.

In *Dombey and Son* there is a very apt comparison
of Mr. Feeder, B.A., to this instrument.   He was

Doctor Blimber's assistant master, and was entrusted with the education of little Paul.

> Mr. Feeder, B.A. . . . was a kind of human barrel-organ with a little list of tunes at which he was continually working, over and over again, without any variation. He might have been fitted up with a change of barrels, perhaps, in early life, if his destiny had been favourable, but it had not been.

So he had only one barrel, his sole occupation being to 'bewilder the young ideas of Dr. Blimber's young gentlemen.' Sometimes he had his Virgil stop on, and at other times his Herodotus stop. In trying to keep up the comparison, however, Dickens makes a curious mistake. In the above quotation Feeder is assigned one barrel only, while in Chapter XLI we are told that he had 'his other barrels on a shelf behind him.'

We find another comparison in *Little Dorrit*, when the long-suffering Pancks turns round on Casby, his employer, and exposes his hypocrisy. Pancks, who has had much difficulty in getting his master's rents from the tenants, makes up his mind to leave him; and before doing so he tells the whole truth about Casby to the inhabitants of Bleeding Heart Yard. 'Here's the Stop,' said Pancks, 'that sets the tune to be ground. And there is but one tune, and its name is "Grind! Grind! Grind!"'

Guitar

Although the guitar was a fashionable instrument sixty years ago, there are but few references to it. This was the instrument that enabled the three Miss Briggses, each of them performers, to eclipse the glory of the Miss Tauntons, who could only manage a harp. On the eventful day of 'The Steam Excursion' (*S. B.*) the three sisters brought their instruments, carefully packed up in dark green cases,

which were carefully stowed away in the bottom of the boat, accompanied by two immense portfolios of music, which it would take at least a week's incessant playing to get through.

At a subsequent stage of the proceedings they were asked to play, and after replacing a broken string, and a vast deal of screwing and tightening, they gave ' a new Spanish composition, for three voices and three guitars,' and secured an encore, thus completely overwhelming their rivals. In the account of the *French Watering-Place* (*R. P.*) we read about a guitar on the pier, ' to which a boy or woman sings without any voice little songs without any tune.'

On one of his night excursions in the guise of an ' Uncommercial Traveller ' Dickens discovered a stranded Spaniard, named Antonio. In response to a general invitation ' the swarthy youth ' takes up his cracked guitar and gives them the ' feeblest ghost of a tune,' while the inmates of the miserable den kept time with their heads.

Dora used to delight David Copperfield by singing enchanting ballads in the French language and accompanying herself ' on a glorified instrument, resembling a guitar,' though subsequent references show it was that instrument and none otler.

We read in *Little Dorrit* that Young John Chivery wore ' pantaloons so highly decorated with side stripes, that each leg was a three-stringed lute.' This appears to be the only reference to this instrument, and a lute of three strings is the novelist's own conception, the usual number being about nine.

CHAPTER IV

VARIOUS INSTRUMENTS (continued)

MANY musical instruments and terms are mentioned by way of illustration. Blathers, the Bow Street officer (*O. T.*), plays carelessly with his handcuffs as if they were a pair of castanets. Miss Miggs (*B. R.*) clanks her pattens as if they were a pair of cymbals. Mr. Bounderby (*H. T.*), during his conversation with Harthouse,

with his hat in his hand, gave a beat upon the crown at every division of his sentences, as if it were a tambourine ;

and in the same work the electric wires rule 'a colossal strip of music-paper out of the evening sky.'

Perhaps the most extraordinary comparison is that instituted by Mrs. Lirriper in reference to her late husband.

My poor Lirriper was a handsome figure of a man, with a beaming eye and a voice as mellow as a musical instrument made of honey and steel.

What a vivid imagination the good woman had !

Her descriptive powers remind us of those possessed by Mrs. Gamp in speaking of the father of the mysterious Mrs. Harris.

As pleasant a singer, Mr. Chuzzlewit, as ever you heerd, with a voice like a Jew's-harp in the bass notes.

There are many humorous references to remarkable performances on various instruments more or less musical in their nature. During the election at Eatanswill the crier performed two concertos on his bell, and shortly afterwards followed them up with a fantasia on the same instrument. Dickens suffered much from church bells, and gives vent to his feelings about them in *Little Dorrit,* where he says that

Maddening church bells of all degrees of dissonance, sharp and flat, cracked and clear, fast and slow, made the brick-and-mortar echoes hideous.

In his *Pictures from Italy* he wrote thus :

At Genoa the bells of the church ring incessantly, not in peals, or any known form of sound, but in horrible, irregular, jerking dingle, dingle, dingle ; with a sudden stop at every fifteenth dingle or so, which is maddening. . . . The noise is supposed to be particularly obnoxious to evil spirits.

But it was these same bells, which he found so maddening, that inspired him with the title of a well-known story. He had chosen a subject, but was at a loss for a name. As he sat working one morning there suddenly rose up from Genoa

the clang and clash of all its steeples, pouring into his ears, again and again, in a tuneless, grating, discordant jerking, hideous vibration that made his ideas spin round and round till they lost themselves in a whirl of vexation and giddiness, and dropped down dead. . . . Only two days later came a letter in which not a syllable was written but ' We have heard THE CHIMES at midnight, Master Shallow,' and I knew he had discovered what he wanted.[1]

Yet, in spite of all this, Dickens shows—through his characters—a deep interest in bells and bell-lore. Little Paul Dombey finds a man mending the clocks at Dr. Blimber's Academy, and asks a multitude of questions about chimes and clocks ; as, whether people watched up in the lonely church steeples by night to make them strike, and how the bells were rung when people died, and whether those were different bells from wedding-bells, or only sounded dismal in the fancies of the living ; and then the precocious small boy proceeds to give the astonished clockmaker some useful information about King Alfred's candles and curfew-bells.

As Smike and Nicholas tramp their long journey

---

[1] Forster, *Life of Charles Dickens.*

to Portsmouth they hear the sheep-bells tinkling on the downs. To Tom Pinch journeying London-wards ' the brass work on the harness was a complete orchestra of little bells.'

What a terror the bells are to Jonas Chuzzlewit just before he starts on his evil journey ! He hears

the ringers practising in a neighbouring church, and the clashing of their bells was almost maddening. Curse the clamouring bells ! they seemed to know that he was listening at the door, and to proclaim it in a crowd of voices to all the town ! Would they never be still ? They ceased at last, and then the silence was so new and terrible that it seemed the prelude to some dreadful noise.

The boom of the bell is associated with many of the villains of the novels. Fagin hears it when under sentence of death. Blackpool and Carker hear the accusing bells when in the midst of planning their evil deeds.

We can read the characters of some by the way they ring a bell. The important little Mr. Bailey, when he goes to see his friend Poll Sweedlepipe (*M. C.*), ' came in at the door with a lunge, to get as much sound out of the bell as possible,' while Bob Sawyer gives a pull as if he would bring it up by the roots. Mr. Clennam pulls the rope with a hasty jerk, and Mr. Watkins Tottle with a faltering jerk, while Tom

Pinch gives a gentle pull.   And how angry Mr.
Mantalini is with Newman Noggs because he keeps
him

'ringing at this confounded old cracked tea-kettle of a bell,
every tinkle of which is enough to throw a strong man into con-
vulsions, upon my life and soul,—oh demmit.'

The introduction of electric bells has been a great
trial to those who used to vent their wrath on the
wire-pulled article or the earlier bell-rope, which used
not infrequently to add unnecessary fuel by coming
incontinently down on the head of the aggrieved one.
What a pull the fierce gentleman must have given
whose acquaintance Mr. Pickwick made when he
was going to Bath ! He had been kept waiting
for his buttered toast, so he (Captain Dowler)

rang the bell with great violence, and told the waiter he'd better
bring the toast in five seconds, or he'd know the reason why.

Dickens rang far more changes on the bells than
there is space to enumerate ; but I have shown to
what extent he makes their sound a commentary
on innumerable phases of life. A slight technical
knowledge of bell phraseology is found in *Barnaby
Rudge* (7), where he mentions the variations known
as a ' triple bob major.' Finally there is an interesting reference in *Master Humphrey's Clock* to a

use of the bell which has now passed into history. Belinda says in a postscript to a letter to Master Humphrey, ' The bellman, rendered impatient by delay, is ringing dreadfully in the passage ' ; while in a second PS. she says, ' I open this to say the bellman is gone, and that you must not expect it till the next post.'

In the old days it was the custom for the letter-carriers to collect letters by ringing a bell.

There is no doubt that a most extraordinary, certainly a most original, musical effect is that secured by Mr. George (*B. H.*), who had just finished smoking.

' Do you know what that tune is, Mr. Smallweed ? ' he adds, after breaking off to whistle one, accompanied on the table with the empty pipe.

' Tune,' replies the old man.   ' No, we never have tunes here.'

' That's the " Dead March " in *Saul*. They bury soldiers to it, so it's the natural end of the subject.'

Surely a highly original way of bringing a conversation to a close !

This march is referred to in *Our Mutual Friend*, where Mr. Wilfer suggests that going through life with Mrs. Wilfer is like keeping time to the ' Dead March ' in *Saul*, from which singular simile we may gather that this lady was not the liveliest of companions.

Several other instruments are casually mentioned. Mr. Hardy (*S.B.T. 7*) was a master of many accomplishments.

He could sing comic songs, imitate hackney coachmen and fowls, play airs on his chin, and execute concertos on the Jew's harp.

The champion ' chin ' performer of the early Victorian period was Michael Boai, ' The celebrated chin melodist,' who was announced to perform ' some of his admired pieces ' at many of the places of entertainment.   There is another reference to this extraordinary way of producing music in *Sketches by Boz*, where Mrs. Tippin performed an air with variations on the guitar, ' accompanied on the chin by Master Tippin.'   To return to Mr. Hardy, this gentleman was evidently deeply interested in all sorts and degrees of music, but he got out of his depth in a conversation with the much-travelled Captain Helves.   After the three Miss Briggses had finished their guitar performances, Mr. Hardy approached the Captain with the question, ' Did you ever hear a Portuguese tambourine ? '

' Did *you* ever hear a tom-tom, sir ? ' sternly inquired the Captain, who lost no opportunity of showing off his travels, real or pretended.

' A what ? ' asked Hardy, rather taken aback.

' A tom-tom.'

' Never.'

' Nor a gum-gum ? '

' Never.'

' What *is* a gum-gum ? ' eagerly inquired several young ladies.

The question is unanswered to this day, though Hardy afterwards suggests it is another name for a humbug.

When Dickens visited the school where the half-time system was in force, he found the boys undergoing military and naval drill. A small boy played the fife while the others went through their exercises. After that a boys' band appeared, the youngsters being dressed in a neat uniform. Then came a choral class, who sang ' the praises of a summer's day to a harmonium.' In the arithmetical exercises the small piper excels (*U. T.* 29).

Wise as the serpent is the four feet of performer on the nearest approach to that instrument.

This was written when the serpent was practically extinct, but Dickens would be very familiar with the name of the instrument, and may have seen and heard it in churches in his younger days.

In referring to another boy's attempt at solving

the arithmetical puzzles, he mentions the cymbals, combined with a faint memory of St. Paul.

I observe the player of the cymbals to dash at a sounding answer now and then rather than not cut in at all; but I take that to be in the way of his instrument.

In *Great Expectations* Mr. Wopsle, who is a parish clerk by profession, had an ambition not only to tread the boards, but to start off as Hamlet. His appearance was not a success, and the audience was derisive.

On his taking the recorders—very like a little black flute that had just been played in the orchestra and handed out at the door—he was called upon unanimously for ' Rule Britannia.'

Reference has already been made to Bucket's music-shop, so we must not forget to visit Caleb Plummer's little room, where there were

scores of melancholy little carts which, when the wheels went round, performed most doleful music. Many small fiddles, drums, and other instruments of torture.

The old man made a rude kind of harp specially for his poor blind daughter, and on which Dot used to play when she visited the toy-maker's. Caleb's musical contribution would be ' a Bacchanalian song, something about a sparkling bowl,' which much annoyed his grumpy employer.

'What! you're singing, are you?' said Tackleton, putting his head in at the door. 'Go it, *I* can't sing.'

Nobody would have suspected him of it. He hadn't what is generally termed a singing face, by any means.

The wonderful duet between the cricket and the kettle at the commencement of *The Cricket on the Hearth* certainly deserves mention, though it is rather difficult to know whether to class the performers as instrumentalists or singers. The kettle began it with a series of short vocal snorts, which at first it checked in the bud, but finally it burst into a stream of song, 'while the lid performed a sort of jig, and clattered like a deaf and dumb cymbal that had never known the use of its twin brother.' Then the cricket came in with its chirp, chirp, chirp, and at it they went in fierce rivalry until 'the kettle, being dead beat, boiled over, and was taken off the fire.'

Dickens was certainly partial to the cricket, for elsewhere (*M. H. C.*) we read of the clock that

makes cheerful music, like one of those chirping insects who delight in the warm hearth.

There are two or three references to the key bugle, which also used to be known as the Kent bugle. It was a popular instrument half a century ago, as the addition of keys gave it a much greater range of notes than the ordinary bugle possessed. A notable though inefficient performer was the driver who took Martin Chuzzlewit up to London.

He was musical, besides, and had a little key bugle in his pocket on which, whenever the conversation flagged, he played the first part of a great many tunes, and regularly broke down in the second

This instrument was on Mr. Feeder's *agenda*. Two more instruments demand our attention. At the marriage of Tackleton and May Fielding (*C. H.*) there were to be marrow-bones and cleavers, while to celebrate the union of Trotty Veck's daughter Meg and Richard they had a band including the aforesaid instruments and also the drum and the bells. It was formerly the custom for butchers' assistants to provide themselves with marrow-bones and cleavers for musical effects. Each cleaver was ground so that when it was struck with the bone it emitted a certain note.[1] A complete band would consist of eight men, with their cleavers so tuned as to give an octave of notes. After more or less practice they would offer their services as bandsmen on the occasion

[1] This is rather a modern development.

of marriage ceremonies, which they had a wonderful faculty for locating, and they would provide music (of a kind) *ad libitum* until the requisite fee was forthcoming. If their services were declined the butchers would turn up all the same, and make things very unpleasant for the marriage party. The custom dates from the eighteenth century, and though it has gradually fallen into disuse a marrow-bone and cleaver band is still available in London for those who want it. A band took part in a wedding ceremony at Clapham as recently as the autumn of 1911.

The following extract, referring to the second marriage of Mr. Dombey, shows what bridal parties had to put up with in the good old days:

The men who play the bells have got scent of the marriage ; and the marrow-bones and cleavers too ; and a brass band too. The first are practising in a back settlement near Battle-bridge[1]; the second put themselves in communication, through their chief, with Mr. Tomlinson, to whom they offer terms to be bought off ; and the third, in the person of an artful trombone, lurks and dodges round the corner, waiting for some traitor-tradesman to reveal the place and hour of breakfast, for a bribe.

Other instruments casually referred to are the Pan's pipes, which in one place is also called a mouth-organ (*S. B. S.* 20), the flageolet, and the

[1] Near King's Cross Station (G.N.R.).

F

triangle.   It is difficult to classify the walking-stick on which Mr. Jennings Rudolph played tunes before he went behind the parlour door and gave his celebrated imitations of actors, edgetools, and animals (*S. B. C.* 8).

CHAPTER V

CHURCH MUSIC

DICKENS has not much to say about church music as such, but the references are interesting, inasmuch as they throw some light upon it during the earlier years of his life. In *Our Parish* (*S. B.*) we read about the old naval officer who

finds fault with the sermon every Sunday, says that the organist ought to be ashamed of himself, and offers to back himself for any amount to sing the psalms better than all the children put together.

This reminds us that during the first half of last century, and indeed later in many places, the church choir as we know it did not exist, and the leading of the singing was entrusted to the children of the charity school under the direction of the clerk, a custom which had existed since the seventeenth century. The chancel was never used for the choir, and the children sat up in the gallery at the west end, on either side of the organ. In a City church that Dickens attended the choir was limited to two girls.

The organ was so out of order that he could ' hear more of the rusty working of the stops than of any music.'   When the service began he was so depressed that, as he says,

I gave but little heed to our dull manner of ambling through the service ; to the brisk clerk's manner of encouraging us to try a note or two at psalm time ; to the gallery congregation's manner of enjoying a shrill duet, without a notion of time or tune ; to the whity-brown man's manner of shutting the minister into the pulpit, and being very particular with the lock of the door, as if he were a dangerous animal.

Elsewhere he found in the choir gallery an ' exhausted charity school ' of four boys and two girls.   The congregations were small, a state of things which at any rate satisfied Mrs. Lirriper, who had a pew at St. Clement Danes and was ' partial to the evening service not too crowded.'

In *Sunday under Three Heads* we have a vivid picture of the state of things at a fashionable church. Carriages roll up, richly dressed people take their places and inspect each other through their glasses.

The organ peals forth, the hired singers commence a short hymn, and the congregation condescendingly rise, stare about them and converse in whispers.

Dickens passes from church to chapel.   Here, he says,

the hymn is sung—not by paid singers, but by the whole assembly at the loudest pitch of their voices, unaccompanied by any musical instrument, the words being given out, two lines at a time, by the clerk.

It cannot be said that, as far as the music is concerned, either of these descriptions is exaggerated when we remember the time at which they were written (1838). Very few chapels in London had organs, or indeed instruments of any kind, and there is no doubt that the congregations, as a rule, *did* sing at the tops of their voices, a proceeding known under the more euphonious title of ' hearty congregational singing.'

He gives a far more favourable account of the music in the village church. In the essay just referred to he mentions the fact that he attended a service in a West of England church where the service ' was spoken—not merely read—by a grey-headed minister.'

The psalms were accompanied by a few instrumental performers, who were stationed in a small gallery extending across the church at the lower end ; and the voices were led by the clerk, who, it was evident, derived no slight pride and gratification from this portion of the service.

But if the church music in England was not of a very high quality when Dickens wrote the above,

it was, according to his own account, far superior to
what he heard in certain churches in Italy.   When
in Rome he visited St. Peter's, where he was quite
unimpressed by the music.

> I have been infinitely more affected in many Engislh cathe-
> drals when the organ has been playing, and in many English
> country churches when the congregation have been singing.

On another occasion he attended church at Genoa
on a feast day, and he writes thus about the music :

> The organ played away lustily, and a full band did the like ;
> while a conductor, in a little gallery opposite the band, ham-
> mered away on the desk before him, with a scroll, and a tenor,
> without any voice, sang.   The band played one way, the organ
> played another, the singer went a third, and the unfortunate
> conductor banged and banged, and flourished his scroll on some
> principle of his own ; apparently well satisfied with the whole
> performance.   I never did hear such a discordant din.

Parish Clerks

We have but few references to parish clerks in the
novels.   Mr. Wopsle (*G. E.*)—whom Mr. Andrew
Lang calls ' one of the best of Dickens' minor
characters'— 'punished the Amens tremendously,'[1]

---

[1] Dickens frequently uses the word in this sense.   Tom Pinch says,
' I shall punish the Boar's Head tremendously.'   It is also interesting
to note that Dickens uses the phrase ' I don't think ' in its modern

and when he gave out the psalms—always giving the whole verse—he looked all round the congregation first, as much as to say ' You have heard our friend overhead ; oblige me with your opinion of this style.' This gentleman subsequently became a ' play-actor,' but failed to achieve the success he desired. Solomon Daisy (*B. R.*) is bell-ringer and parish clerk of Chigwell, though we hear nothing of his exploits in these capacities. However, he must have been a familiar figure to the villagers as he stood in his little desk on the Sunday, giving out the psalms and leading the singing, because when in the rifled and dismantled Maypole he appeals to the poor witless old Willet as to whether he did not know him—

' You know us, don't you, Johnny ? ' said the little clerk, rapping himself on the breast. ' Daisy, you know—Chigwell Church—bell-ringer—little desk on Sundays—eh, Johnny ? '

Mr. Willet reflected for a few moments, and then muttered as it were mechanically : ' Let us sing to the praise and glory of——'

' Yes, to be sure,' cried the little man hastily, ' that's it, that's me, Johnny.'

---

slang meaning on at least two occasions. Tom Pinch remarks ' I'm a nice man, I don't think, as John used to say ' (*M. C.* 6), and Sam Weller (*P. P.* 38) says to Mr. Winkle ' you're a amiably-disposed young man, sir, I don't think.' Mark Tapley uses the expression ' a pious fraud ' (*M. C.* 13).

Besides the numerous body of more or less distinguished artists whom the novelist introduces to us and whose achievements are duly set forth in these pages, there are two others whose connexion with Cloisterham gives them a prominent position in our list.   One of these is the Rev. Mr. Crisparkle (*E. D.*), Minor Canon of Cloisterham :

early riser, musical, classical, cheerful, kind, good-natured, social, contented, and boy-like.

What a contrast to the Stiggins and Chadband type !   He is a member of the ' Alternate Musical Wednesdays ' Society, and amongst his lesser duties is that of corrector-in-chief of the un-Dean-like English of the cathedral verger.

It is Mr. Crisparkle's custom to sit up last of the early house-hold, very softly touching his piano and practising his parts in concerted vocal music.

Over a closet in his dining-room, where occasional refreshments were kept,

a portrait of Handel in a flowing wig beamed down at the specta-tor, with a knowing air of being up to the contents of the closet, and a musical air of intending to combine all its harmonies in one delicious fugue.

The Minor Canon is a warm admirer of Jasper's

musical talents, and on one occasion in particular is much impressed with his singing.

I must thank you, Jasper, for the pleasure with which I have heard you to-day.   Beautiful ! Delightful !

And thus we are introduced to the other musician, whose position at Cloisterham Cathedral is almost as much a mystery as that of Edwin Drood himself. He was the lay precentor or lay clerk, and he was also a good choirmaster.   It is unnecessary to criticize or examine too closely the exact position that Jasper held.   In answer to a question on this subject, Mr. B. Luard-Selby, the present organist of Rochester Cathedral, writes thus :

We have never had in the choir of Rochester Cathedral such a musical functionary as Dickens describes in *The Mystery of Edwin Drood*.   The only person approaching Jasper in the choir is one of the lay clerks who looks after the music, but who of course has nothing to do with *setting* the music for the month. I don't think Dickens had much idea of church order or of cathedral worship, though he may have gone over the cathedral with a verger on occasions.   The music of a cathedral is always in the hands of the precentor, assisted by the organist.

It is Edwin Drood himself who says that Jasper was lay precentor or lay clerk at the cathedral. He had a great reputation as a choir-trainer and teacher of music, but he is already weary of his position and takes little notice of words of eulogy. He was well acquainted with the old melodies, and on one occasion we find him sitting at the piano singing brave songs to Mr. Sapsea.

> No kickshaw ditties, favourites with national enemies, but . . . genuine George the Third home brewed, exhorting him (as ' my brave boys ') to reduce to a smashed condition all other islands but this island, and all continents, peninsulas, isthmuses, promontories, and other geographical forms of land soever, besides sweeping the sea in all directions.   In short he rendered it pretty clear that Providence made a distinct mistake in originating so small a nation of hearts of oak, and so many other verminous peoples.

We have a different picture of him on another occasion, as he sits ' chanting choir music in a low and beautiful voice, for two or three hours '—a somewhat unusual exercise even for the most enthusiastic choirmaster.   But this was before the strange journey with Durdles, and we can only guess at the weird thoughts which were passing through the musician's mind as he sat in his lonely room.

We have only a brief reference to the choir of Cloisterham Cathedral.   Towards the end we read of them ' struggling into their nightgowns ' before the service, while they subsequently are ' as much in a hurry to get their bedgowns off as they were

but now to get them on '—and these were almost
the last words that came from the Master's pen.

Anthems

There is an interesting reference to anthems in
connexion with the Foundling Hospital,[1] an institu-
tion which Dickens mentions several times. Mr.
Wilding (*N. T.*), after he had been pumped
on by his lawyer in order to clear his head, names
the composers of the anthems he had been accustomed to sing at the Foundling.

Handel, Mozart, Haydn, Kent, Purcell, Doctor Arne, Greene,
Mendelssohn. I know the choruses to those anthems by heart.
Foundling Chapel collection.

Mr. Wilding had a scheme of forming his household retainers and dependents into a singing-class in
the warehouse, and a choir in the neighbouring
church. Only one member, Joey Ladle, refused to
join, for fear he should ' muddle the ' armony,' and
his remark that

Handel must have been down in some of them foreign cellars
pretty much for to go and say the same thing so many times
over

is certainly not lacking in originality.

[1] 'Pet' (*L. D.* 2) was a frequent visitor to the Hospital.

Hymns and Hymn-Tunes

There are many purists in church music who object to adaptations of any kind, and we do not know what their feelings are on reading the account of the meeting of the Brick Lane Branch of the United Grand Junction Ebenezer Temperance Association. In order to vary the proceedings Mr. Anthony Humm announced that

Brother Mordlin had adapted the beautiful words of 'Who hasn't heard of a Jolly Young Waterman' to the tune of the Old Hundredth, which he would request them to join in singing. (Great applause.) And so the song commenced, the chairman giving out two lines at a time, in proper orthodox fashion.

It was this air that Mr. Jerry's dog, as already related, ground out of the barrel-organ, but, besides this particular melody, we do not find that Dickens mentions any other hymn-tune. The hymns referred to are rather more in number. In *The Wreck of the Golden Mary* Mrs. Atherfield sang Little Lucy to sleep with the Evening Hymn. There is a veiled reference to Ken's Morning Hymn in *O. C. S.*, where Sampson Brass says :

'Here we are, Mr. Richard, rising with the sun to run our little course—our course of duty, sir.'

Dr. Watts makes several appearances. Dickens

made the acquaintance of this noted hymnist in
early youth (see p. 7), and makes good use of his
knowledge. In *The Cricket on the Hearth* Mrs.
Peerybingle asks John if he ever learnt ' How doth
the little ' when he went to school. ' Not to quite
know it,' John returned. ' I was very near it once.'
Another of the Doctor's hymns is suggested by the
behaviour of the Young Tetterbys (*H. M.*).

The contentions between the Tetterbys' children for the milk
and water jug, common to all, which stood upon the table,
presented so lamentable an instance of angry passions risen
very high indeed, that it was an outrage on the memory of Dr.
Watts.

The pages of history abound with instances of
misguided amateurs who have amended the hymns
(and tunes) of others in order to bring them into
their way of thinking, and a prominent place in
their ranks must be assigned to Miss Monflathers
(*O. C. S.*), who managed to parody the good Doctor's
meaning to an alarming extent and to insist that

In books, or work or healthful play [1]

is only applicable to *genteel* children, while all poor
people's children, such as Little Nell, should spend
their time

[1] From the poem on *Industry*.

> In work, work, work. In work alway,
>   Let my first years be passed,
> That I may give for ev'ry day
>   Some good account at last,

which is far from the good Doctor's meaning.

Dr. Strong, David Copperfield's second school-master, was fond of quoting this great authority on mischief, but Mr. Wickfield suggests that Dr. Watts, had he known mankind well, would also have written ' Satan finds some mischief still for busy hands to do.'

Some years ago a question was raised in *Notes and Queries* as to the identity of the ' No. 4 Collection ' of hymns which appeared to afford consolation to Job Trotter. No answer was vouchsafed, the fact being that the title is a pure invention, and no such collection has ever existed. It is scarcely necessary to add that history is silent as to the identity of the hymn-book which Uriah Heep was reading when David Copperfield and others visited him in prison.

We are indebted to Dickens for the introduction to the literary world of Adelaide Procter, many of whose sacred verses have found their way into our hymnals. The novelist wrote an introduction to her *Legends and Lyrics*, in which he tells the story of how, as editor of *Household Words*, he accepted

verses sent him from time to time by a Miss Mary
Berwick, and only discovered, some months later,
that his contributor was the daughter of his friend
Procter, who was known under the *nom de plume* of
Barry Cornwall.

There seems to be some difficulty in regard to
the authorship of the hymn

> Hear my prayer, O Heavenly Father,
> Ere I lay me down to sleep ;
> Bid Thy angels, pure and holy,
> Round my bed their vigil keep.

It has already been pointed out (see *Choir*, February, 1912) that this hymn appeared in the
Christmas number of *Household Words* for 1856, in
a story entitled *The Wreck of the Golden Mary*.
The chief authorities on the works of Dickens claim
it as his composition, and include it in his collected
works. On the other hand, Miller, in his *Our Hymns*
(1866), states that Miss Harriet Parr informed him
that the hymn, and the story of *Poor Dick*, in which
it occurs, were both her own. We may add that
when Dr. Allon applied for permission to include
it in his new hymn-book Dickens referred him to the
authoress.

Dr. Julian takes this as authoritative, and has no

hesitation in ascribing the hymn to Miss Parr. On the other hand, Forster records in his *Life of Dickens* that a clergyman, the Rev. R. H. Davies, had been struck by this hymn when it appeared in *Household Words*, and wrote to thank him for it. ' I beg to thank you,' Dickens answered (Christmas Eve, 1856), 'for your very acceptable letter, not the less because I am myself the writer you refer to.' Here Dickens seems to claim the authorship, but it is possible he was referring to something else in the magazine when he wrote these words, and not to the hymn.

CHAPTER VI

SONGS AND SOME SINGERS

THE numerous songs and vocal works referred to by Dickens in his novels and other writings furnish perhaps the most interesting, certainly the most instructive, branch of this subject. His knowledge of song and ballad literature was extraordinary, and he did not fail to make good use of it. Not only are the quotations always well chosen and to the point, but the use of them has greatly added to the interest of such characters as Swiveller, Micawber, Cuttle, and many others, all of whom are of a very musical turn of mind. These songs may be conveniently divided into three classes, the first containing the national and popular airs of the eighteenth century, of which ' Rule Britannia ' and ' Sally in our Alley ' are notable examples. Many of these are referred to in the following pages, while a full list will be found on pp. 135–163.

I.—*National Songs*

There are numerous references to ' Rule Britannia.' Besides those mentioned elsewhere we have

G

the picture of little David Copperfield in his dismal
home.

What evenings when the candles came, and I was expected
to employ myself, but not daring to read an entertaining book,
pored over some hard-headed, harder-hearted treatise on arith-
metic ; when the tables of weights and measures set themselves
to tunes as ' Rule Britannia,' or ' Away with Melancholy ' !

No wonder he finally went to sleep over them!

In *Dombey and Son* Old Sol has a wonderful story
of the *Charming Sally* being wrecked in the Baltic,
while the crew sang ' Rule Britannia ' as the ship
went down, ' ending with one awful scream in
chorus.' Walter gives the date of the tragedy as
1749. (The song was written in 1740.)

Captain Cuttle had a theory that ' Rule Britannia,' ' which the garden angels sang about so many
times over,' embodied the outlines of the British
Constitution. It is perhaps unnecessary to explain
that the Captain's ' garden angels ' appear in the
song as ' guardian angels.'

Mark Tapley, when in America, entertained a
grey-haired black man by whistling this tune with
all his might and main. The entry of Martin
Chuzzlewit caused him to stop the tune

at that point where Britons generally are supposed to declare
(when it is whistled) that they never, never, never——

In the article on ' Wapping Workhouse' (*U. T.*) Dickens introduces the first verse of the song in criticizing the workhouse system and its treatment of old people, and in the *American Notes* he tells us that he left Canada with ' Rule Britannia ' sounding in his ears.

' British Grenadiers,' said Mr. Bucket to Mr. Bagnet, ' there's a tune to warm an Englishman up ! *Could* you give us " British Grenadiers," my fine fellow ? ' And the ' fine fellow,' who was none other than Bagnet junior (also known as ' Woolwich '), promptly

fetches his fife and performs the stirring melody, during which performance Mr. Bucket, much enlivened, beats time, and never fails to come in sharp with the burden ' Brit Ish Gra-a-anadeers.'

Our national anthem is frequently referred to. In the description of the public dinner (*S. B. S.* 19)—

' God Save the Queen ' is sung by the professional gentlemen, the unprofessional gentlemen joining in the chorus, and giving the national anthem an effect which the newspapers, with great justice, describe as ' perfectly electrical.'

On another occasion we are told the company, sang the national anthem with national independence, each one singing it according to his own ideas of time and tune.   This is the usual way of singing it at the present day.

In addition to those above mentioned we find references to 'The Marseillaise' and 'Ça ira,' both of which Dickens says he heard in Paris.   In *Little Dorrit* Mr. Meagles says :

As to Marseilles, we know what Marseilles is.   It sent the most insurrectionary tune into the world that was ever composed.

Without disputing the decided opinion expressed by the speaker, there is no doubt that some would give the palm to 'Ça ira,' which the novelist refers to in one of his letters.   The words of this song were adapted in 1790 to the tune of 'Carillon National.'   This was a favourite air of Marie Antoinette, and she frequently played it on the harpsichord.   After her downfall she heard it as a cry of hatred against herself—it followed her from Versailles to the capital, and she would hear it from her prison and even when going to her death.

When Martin Chuzzlewit and Mark Tapley were on their way to America, one of their fellow travellers was

an English gentleman who was strongly suspected of having run away from a bank, with something in his possession belonging to its strong-box besides the key [and who] grew eloquent

upon the subject of the rights of man, and hummed the
Marseillaise Hymn constantly.

In an article on this tune in the *Choir* (Nov., 1911)
it is stated that it was composed in 1792 at Strasburg,
but received its name from the fact that a band of
soldiers going from Marseilles to Paris made the new
melody their marching tune.   A casual note about
it appears to be the only musical reference in *A Tale
of Two Cities.*

From America we have ' Hail Columbia ' and
' Yankee Doodle.'   In *Martin Chuzzlewit* we meet
the musical coach-driver who played snatches of
tunes on the key bugle.   A friend of his went to
America, and wrote home saying he was always
singing ' Ale Columbia.'   In his *American Notes*
Dickens tells about a Cleveland newspaper which
announced that America had ' whipped England
twice, and that soon they would sing " Yankee
Doodle " in Hyde Park and " Hail Columbia " in
the scarlet courts of Westminster.'

II.—*Songs from* 1780–1840

We then come to a group of songs dating,
roughly, from 1780.   This includes several popular

sea songs by Charles Dibdin and others, some
ballad opera airs, the *Irish Melodies* and other
songs by Thomas Moore, and a few sentimental
ditties. Following these we have the songs
of the early Victorian period, consisting of
more sentimental ditties of a somewhat feebler
type, with a few comic and nigger minstrel
songs. The task of identifying the numerous songs
referred to has been interesting, but by no means
easy. No one who has not had occasion to refer
to them can have any idea of the hundreds, nay,
of the thousands, of song-books that were turned
out from the various presses under an infinitude of
titles during the eighteenth and early nineteenth
centuries. There is nothing like them at the present
day, and the reasons for their publication have long
ceased to exist. It should be explained that the
great majority of these books contained the words
only, very few of them being furnished with
the musical notes. Dickens has made use of con-
siderably over a hundred different songs. In
some cases the references are somewhat obscure,
but their elucidation is necessary to a proper
understanding of the text. An example of this
occurs in Chapter IX of *Martin Chuzzlewit,*
where we are told the history of the various

names given to the young red-haired boots at
Mrs. Todgers' commercial boarding-house. When
the Pecksniffs visited the house

he was generally known among the gentlemen as Bailey Junior,
a name bestowed upon him in contradistinction perhaps to Old
Bailey, and possibly as involving the recollection of an unfortunate lady of the same name, who perished by her own hand
early in life and has been immortalized in a ballad.

The song referred to here is ' Unfortunate Miss
Bailey,' by George Colman, and sung by Mr.
Mathews in the comic opera of *Love Laughs at
Locksmiths*. It tells the story of a maid who hung
herself, while her persecutor took to drinking
ratafia.

Dickens often refers to these old song-books,
either under real or imaginary names. Captain
Cuttle gives ' Stanfell's Budget ' as the authority for
one of his songs, and this was probably the song-book
that formed one of the ornaments which he placed
in the room he was preparing for Florence Dombey.
Other common titles are the ' Prentice's Warbler,'
which Simon Tappertit used, ' Fairburn's Comic
Songster,' and the ' Little Warbler,' which is mentioned two or three times. Of the songs belonging to
this second period, some are embedded in ballad
operas and plays, popular enough in their day, but

long since forgotten. An example is Mr. Jingle's quotation when he tells the blushing Rachel that he is going

> In hurry, post haste for a licence,
>   In hurry, ding dong I come back,

though he omitted the last two lines :

> For that you shan't need bid me twice hence,
>   I'll be here and there in a crack.

This verse is sung by Lord Grizzle in Fielding's *Tom Thumb*, as arranged by Kane O'Hara.

Paul and Virginia is mentioned by Mrs. Flora Finching (*L. D.*) as being one of the things that ought to have been returned to Arthur Clennam when their engagement was broken off. This was a ballad opera by Reeve and Mazzinghi, and the opening number is the popular duet ' See from ocean rising,' concerning which there is a humorous passage in ' The Steam Excursion ' (*S. B.*), where it is sung by one of the Miss Tauntons and Captain Helves. The last-named, ' after a great deal of preparatory crowing and humming,' began

in that grunting tone in which a man gets down, heaven knows where, without the remotest chance of ever getting up again. This in private circles is frequently designated a ' bass voice.'

See from o - cean ris - ing Bright flame, the orb of day;

From yon grove the var - ied song Shall slum-ber from Virgin - ia

chase, chase a-way, Slum ber from Vir-gin - ia chase, chase a-way.

Dickens is not quite correct in this description, as the part of Paul was created by Incledon, the celebrated tenor, but there are still to be found basses who insist on singing tenor when they think that part wants their assistance.

III.—*Contemporary Comic Songs*

When Dickens visited Vauxhall (*S. B. S.* 14) in 1836, he heard a variety entertainment, to which some reference has already been made. Amongst the performers was a comic singer who bore the name of one of the English counties, and who

sang a very good song about the seven ages, the first half hour of which afforded the assembly the purest delight.

The name of this singer was Mr. Bedford, though

there was also a Mr. Buckingham in the Vauxhall programmes of those days. There are at least four songs, all of them lengthy, though not to the extent Dickens suggests, which bear on the subject. They are :

1.—' All the World's a Stage,' a popular medley written by Mr. L. Rede, and sung by Mrs. Kelley in the *Frolic of the Fairies*.

2.—' Paddy McShane's Seven Ages,' sung by Mr. Johnstone at Drury Lane.

3.—' The Seven Ages,' as sung by Mr. Fuller (eight very long verses).

4.—' The Seven Ages of Woman,' as sung by Mr. Harley.

> You've heard the seven ages of great Mister Man,
> And now Mistress Woman's I'll chaunt, if I can.

This was also a very long song, each verse being sung to a different tune.

Some of these songs are found in a scarce book called *London Oddities* (1822), which also contains ' Time of Day,' probably the comic duet referred to in *The Mistaken Milliner* (S. B.). This sketch was written in 1835 for *Bell's Life in London*, the original title being *The Vocal Dressmaker*, and contains an account of a concert (real or imaginary) at the White Conduit House. This place of entertainment was situated in Penton Street, Islington, near the top of Pentonville Road, and when Dickens wrote his sketch the place had been in existence nearly a hundred years. Early in the nineteenth century it became a place of varied amusements, from balloon ascents to comic songs. Dickens visited the place about 1835. The titles of some of the pieces he mentions as having been sung there are real, while others (such as ' Red Ruffian, retire ') appear to be invented.

Of a different kind is the one sung by the giant Pickleson, known in the profession as Rinaldo di Vasco, a character introduced to us by Dr. Marigold.

> I gave him sixpence (for he was kept as short as he was long), and he laid it out on two three penn'or hs of gin-and-water, which so brisked him up that he sang the favourite comic of ' Shivery Shakey, ain't it cold ? '

Perhaps in no direction does the taste of the British public change so rapidly and so completely as in their idea of humour as depicted in the comic song, and it is unlikely that what passed for humour sixty years ago would appeal to an audience of the

present day.   The song here referred to had a great
though brief popularity.   This is the first verse :

THE MAN THAT COULDN'T GET WARM.

Words by J. Beuler.   *Accompaniment by J. Clinton.*

All you who're fond in spite of price
Of pastry, cream and jellies nice
Be cautious how you take an ice
 Whenever you're overwarm.
A merchant who from India came,
And Shiverand Shakey was his name,
A pastrycook's did once entice
To take a cooling, luscious ice,
The weather, hot enough to kill,
Kept tempting him to eat, until
It gave his corpus such a chill
 He never again felt warm.
Shiverand Shakey O, O, O,
Criminy Crikey ! Isn't it cold,
Woo, woo, woo, oo, oo,
 Behold the man that couldn't get warm.

Some people affect to despise a comic song, but
there are instances where a good specimen has helped
to make history, or has added a popular phrase to
our language.   An instance of the latter is Mac-
Dermott's ' Jingo ' song ' We don't want to fight
but by Jingo if we do.'   An illustration of the former
comes from the coal strike of March, 1912, during

which period the price of that commodity only once
passed the figure it reached in 1875, as we gather from
the old song ' Look at the price of coals.'

> We don't know what's to be done,
> They're forty-two shillings a ton.

There are two interesting references in a song
which Mrs. Jarley's poet adapted to the purposes of
the Waxwork Exhibition, ' If I'd a donkey as
wouldn't go.' The first verse of the song is as
follows :

> If I'd a donkey wot wouldn't go,
> D'ye think I'd wollop him ? No, no, no ;
> But gentle means I'd try, d'ye see,
> Because I hate all cruelty.
> If all had been like me in fact,
> There'd ha' been no occasion for Martin's Act
> Dumb animals to prevent getting crackt
>   On the head, for—
> If I had a donkey wot wouldn't go,
> I never would wollop him, no, no, no ;
> I'd give him some hay, and cry gee O,
>   And come up Neddy.

The singer then meets ' Bill Burns,' who, ' while
crying out his greens,' is ill-treating his donkey.
On being interfered with, Bill Burns says,

> ' You're one of these Mr. Martin chaps '

Then there was a fight, when the 'New Police' came up and 'hiked' them off before the magistrate. There is a satisfactory ending, and 'Bill got fin'd.' Here is a reminder that we are indebted to Mr. Martin, M.P., for initiating the movement which resulted in the 'Royal Society for the Prevention of Cruelty to Animals' being established in 1824. Two years previously Parliament had passed what is known as Martin's Act (1822), which was the first step taken by this or any other country for the protection of animals. In Scene 7 of *Sketches by Boz* there is a mention of 'the renowned Mr. Martin, of coster-monger notoriety.' The reference to the New Police Act reminds us that the London police force was remodelled by Mr. (afterwards Sir Robert) Peel in 1829. Hence the date of the song will be within a year or two of this.

Mr. Reginald Wilfer (*O. M. F.*) owed his nickname to the conventional chorus of some of the comic songs of the period. Being a modest man, he felt unable to live up to the grandeur of his christian name, so he always signed himself 'R. Wilfer.' Hence his neighbours provided him with all sorts of fancy names beginning with R, but his popular name was Rumty, which a 'gentleman of convivial habits connected with the drug market' had

bestowed upon him, and which was derived from
the burden—

> Rumty iddity, row dow dow,
> Sing toodlely teedlely, bow wow wow.

The third decade of the nineteenth century saw
the coming of the Christy Minstrels. One of the
earliest of the so-called ' negro ' impersonators was
T. D. Rice, whose song ' Jim Crow ' (*A. N.*) took
England by storm. It is useless to attempt to
account for the remarkable popularity of this and
many another favourite, but the fact remains that
the song sold by thousands. In this case it may
have been due to the extraordinary antics of the
singer, for the words certainly do not carry
weight (see p. 146).

Rice made his first appearance at the Surrey
Theatre in 1836, when he played in a sketch entitled
Bone Squash Diabolo, in which he took the part of
' Jim Crow.' The song soon went all over England,
and ' Jim Crow ' hats and pipes were all the rage,
while *Punch* caricatured a statesman who changed
his opinions on some question of the day as the
political ' Jim Crow.' To this class also belongs the
song ' Buffalo Gals ' (see p. 10).

Amongst the contents of the shop window at

the watering-place referred to in *Out of the Season* was

every polka with a coloured frontispiece that ever was published ; from the original one, where a smooth male or female
Pole of high rank are coming at the observer with their arms
akimbo, to the ' Ratcatcher's Daughter.'

This last piece is of some slight interest from the fact
that certain people have claimed that the hymn-tune
' Belmont ' is derived therefrom.   We give the first
four lines, and leave our readers to draw their own
conclusions.   It is worth while stating that the first
appearance of the hymn-tune took place soon
after the song became popular.[1]

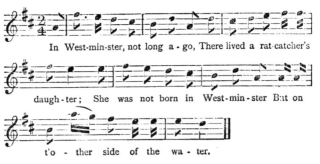

In West-min-ster, not long a - go, There lived a rat-catcher's

daugh-ter;   She was not born in West-min-ster But on

t'o - ther side of the wa - ter.

[1] Mr. Alfred Payne writes thus : ' Some time ago an old friend told
me that he had heard from a Hertfordshire organist that Dr. W. H.
Monk (editor of *Hymns Ancient and Modern*) adapted " Belmont "
from the highly classical melody of which a few bars are given above·
Monk showed this gentleman the notes, being the actual arrangement
he had made from this once popular song, back in the fifties.   This
certainly coincides with its appearance in Severn's *Islington Collection*,
1854.'—See *Hymn-Tunes and their Story*, p. 354.

Some Singers

In the *Pickwick Papers* we have at least three original poems. Wardle's carol—

> I care not for Spring ; on his fickle wing
> Let the blossoms and buds be borne—

has been set to music, but Dickens always preferred that it should be sung to the tune of ' Old King Cole,' though a little ingenuity is required to make it fit in. The ' wild and beautiful legend,'

> Bold Turpin vunce, on Hounslow Heath
> His bold mare Bess bestrode—er,

with which Sam Weller favoured a small but select company on a memorable occasion appears to have been overlooked by composers until Sir Frederick Bridge set it to excellent music. It will be remembered that Sam intimated that he was not

wery much in the habit o' singin' without the instrument; but anythin' for a quiet life, as the man said wen he took the sitiva tion at the lighthouse.

Sam was certainly more obliging than another member of the company, the ' mottled-faced ' gentleman, who, when asked to sing, sturdily and somewhat offensively declined to do so. We also find

H

references to other crusty individuals who flatly refuse to exercise their talents, as, for instance, after the accident to the coach which was conveying Nicholas Nickleby and Squeers to Yorkshire. In response to the call for a song to pass the time away, some protest they cannot, others wish they could, others can do nothing without the book, while the ' very fastidious lady entirely ignored the invitation to give them some little Italian thing out of the last opera.' A somewhat original plea for refusing to sing when asked is given by the chairman of the musical gathering at the Magpie and Stump (*P. P.*). When asked why he won't enliven the company he replies, ' I only know one song, and I have sung it already, and it's a fine of glasses round to sing the same song twice in one night.' Doubtless he was deeply thankful to Mr. Pickwick for changing the subject. At another gathering of a similar nature, we are told about a man who knew a song of seven verses, but he couldn't recall them at the moment, so he sang the first verse seven times.

There is no record as to what the comic duets were that Sam Weller and Bob Sawyer sang in the dickey of the coach that was taking the party to Birmingham, and this suggests what a number of singers of all kinds are referred to, though no

mention is made of their songs. What was Little
Nell's repertoire ? It must have been an extensive
one according to the man in the boat (*O. C. S.* 43).

' You've got a very pretty voice ' . . . said this gentleman.
. . . ' Let me hear a song this minute.'

' I don't think I know one, sir,' returned Nell.

' You know forty-seven songs,' said the man, with a gravity
which admitted of no altercation on the subject. ' Forty-seven's
your number.'

And so the poor little maid had to keep her rough companions
in good humour all through the night.

Then Tiny Tim had a song about a lost child
travelling in the snow ; the miner sang a Christmas
song—' it had been a very old song when he was a
boy,' while the man in the lighthouse (*C. C.*) consoled
himself in his solitude with a 'sturdy' ditty. What
was John Browdie's north-country song ? (*N. N.*).
All we are told is that he took some time to con-
sider the words, in which operation his wife assisted
him, and then

began to roar a meek sentiment (supposed to be uttered by a
gentle swain fast pining away with love and despair) in a voice
of thunder.

The Miss Pecksniffs used to come singing into the
room, but their songs are unrecorded, as well as those
that Florence Dombey used to sing to Paul, to his

great delight.   What was the song Miss Mills sang to David Copperfield and Dora

about the slumbering echoes in the cavern of Memory ; as if she was a hundred years old.

When we first meet Mark Tapley he is singing merrily, and there are dozens of others who sing either for their own delight or to please others. Even old Fips, of Austin Friars, the dry-as-dust lawyer, sang songs to the delight of the company gathered round the festive board in Martin Chuzzlewit's rooms in the Temple.   Truly Dickens must have loved music greatly himself to have distributed such a love of it amongst his characters.

It is not to be expected that Sampson Brass would be musical, and we are not surprised when on an occasion already referred to we find him

humming in a voice that was anything but musical certain vocal snatches which appeared to have reference to the uni n between Church and State, inasmuch as they were compounded of the Evening Hymn and ' God Save the King.'

Whatever music he had in him must have been of a sub-conscious nature, for shortly afterwards he affirms that

the still small voice is a-singing comic songs within me, and all is happiness and joy.

His sister Sally is not a songster, nor is Quilp, though he quotes ' Sally in our Alley ' in reference to the former. All we know about his musical attainments is that he

occasionally entertained himself with a melodious howl, intended for a song but bearing not the faintest resemblance to any scrap of any piece of music, vocal or instrumental, ever invented by man.

Bass singers, and especially the Basso Profundos, will be glad to know that Dickens pays more attention to them than to the other voices, though it must be acknowledged that the references are of a humorous nature. ' Bass ! ' as the young gentleman in one of the *Sketches* remarks to his companion about the little man in the chair, ' bass ! I believe you. He can go down lower than any man ; so low sometimes that you can't hear him.'

And so he does. To hear him growling away, gradually lower and lower down, till he can't get back again, is the most delightful thing in the world.

Of similar calibre is the voice of Captain Helves, already referred to on p. 62.

Topper, who had his eye on one of Scrooge's niece's sisters (*C. C.*),

could growl away in the bass like a good one, and never swell the large veins in his forehead or get red in the face over it.

Dickens must certainly have had much experience of basses, as he seems to know their habits and eccentricities so thoroughly.   In fact it seems to suggest that at some unknown period of his career, hitherto unchronicled by his biographers, he must have been a choirmaster.

He also shows a knowledge of the style of song the basses delighted in

at the harmony meetings in which the collegians at the Marshalsea[1] used to indulge.   Occasionally a vocal strain more sonorous than the generality informed the listener that some boastful bass was in blue water or the hun ing field, or with the reindeer, or on the mountain, or among the heather, but the Marshal of the Marshalsea knew better, and had got him hard and fast.

We are not told what the duet was that Dickens heard at Vauxhall, but the description is certainly vivid enough :

It was a beautiful duet ; first the small gentleman asked a question and then the tall lady answered it ; then the small gentleman and the tall lady sang together most melodiously ; then the small gentleman went through a little piece of vehemence by himself, and got very tenor indeed, in the excitement of his feelings, to which the tall lady responded in a similar manner ; then the small gentleman had a shake or two, after which the tall

---

[1] The Marshalsea was a debtors' prison formerly situated in Southwark.   It was closed about the middle of the last century, and demolished in 1856.

lady had the same, and then they both merged imperceptibly into the original air.

Our author is quite impartial in his distribution of his voices. In *P. P.* we read of a boy of fourteen who was a tenor (not the fat boy), while the quality of the female voices is usually left to the imagination.

If Mrs. Plornish (*L. D.*) is to be believed, her father, Mr. John Edward Nandy, was a remarkable singer. He was

a poor little reedy piping old gentleman, like a worn-out bird, who had been in what he called the music-binding business.

But Mrs. P. was very proud of her father's talents, and in response to her invitation, ' Sing us a song, father,'

Then would he give them Chloe, and if he were in pretty good spirits, Phyllis also—Strephon he had hardly been up to since he went into retirement—and then would Mrs. Plornish declare she did believe there never was such a singer as father, and wipe her eyes.

Old Nandy evidently favoured the eighteenth-century songs, in which the characters here referred to were constantly occurring. At a subsequent period of his history Nandy's vocal efforts surprised even his daughter.

' You never heard father in such voice as he is at present,'
said Mrs. Plornish, her own voice quavering, she was so proud and
pleased.   ' He gave us Strephon last night, to that degree that
Plornish gets up and makes him this speech across the table,
" John Edward Nandy," says Plornish to father, " I never
heard you come the warbles as I have heard you come the
warbles this night."   Ain't it gratifying, Mr. Pancks, though ;
really.'

The Mr. Pancks here referred to did not mind
taking his part in a bit of singing.   He says, in
reference to a ' Harmony evening ' at the Marshalsea :

' I am spending the evening with the rest of 'em,' said Pancks.
' I've been singing.   I've been taking a part in " White Sand
and Grey Sand."   I don't know anything about it.   Never
mind.   I'll take part in anything.   It's all the same, if you're
loud enough.'

Here we have a round of considerable antiquity,
though the date and author are alike unknown.

Glee-Singing

A feature of the Harmonic Meetings at the ' Sol ' (*B. H.*) was the performance of Little Swills, who, after entertaining the company with comic songs, took the ' gruff line ' in a concerted piece, and adjured ' his friends to listen, listen, listen to the wa-ter-fall ! ' Little Swills was also an adept at ' patter and gags.' Glee and catch singing was a feature at the Christmas party given by Scrooge's nephew, for ' they were a musical family, and knew what they were about.' This remark can scarcely be applied to the Malderton family, who, assisted by the redoubtable Mr. Horatio Sparkins,

tried over glees and trios without number ; they having made the pleasing discovery that their voices harmonized beautifully. To be sure, they all sang the first part ; and Horatio, in addition to the slight drawback of having no ear, was perfectly innocent of knowing a note of music ; still, they passed the time very agreeably.

Glee-singing seems to have been a feature in the social life of Cloisterham (*E. D.*).

' We shall miss you, Jasper ' (said Mr. Crisparkle), ' at the " Alternate Musical Wednesdays " to-night ; but no doubt you are best at home. Good-night, God bless you. " Tell me shepherds te-e-ell me : tell me-e-e have you seen (have you seen, have you seen, have you seen) my-y-y Flo-o-ora-a pass this way ! " '

It was a different kind of glee party that left the Blue Boar after the festivities in connexion with Pip's indentures (*G. E.*).

> They were all in excellent spirits on the road home, and sang 'O Lady Fair,' Mr. Wopsle taking the bass, and assisting with a tremendously strong voice (in reply to the inquisitive bore who leads that piece of music in a most impertinent manner by wanting to know all about everybody's private affairs) that *he* was the man with his white locks flowing, and that he was upon the whole the weakest pilgrim going.

Perhaps the most remarkable glee party that Dickens gives us is the one organized by the male boarders at Mrs. Todgers', with a view to serenading the two Miss Pecksniffs.

> It was very affecting, very.   Nothing more dismal could have been desired by the most fastidious taste.   The gentleman of a vocal turn was head mute, or chief mourner; Jinkins took the bass, and the rest took anything they could get. . . . If the two Miss Pecksniffs and Mrs. Todgers had perished by spontaneous combustion, and the serenade had been in honour of their ashes, it would have been impossible to surpass the unutterable despair expressed in that one chorus: 'Go where glory waits thee.'   It was a requiem, a dirge, a moan, a howl, a wail, a lament, an abstract of everything that is sorrowful and hideous in sound.

The song which the literary boarder had written for the occasion, 'All hail to the vessel of Pecksniff, the sire,' is a parody of Scott's 'All hail to the chief who in triumph advances,' from the *Lady of the Lake.*

Two words that by themselves have a musical meaning are ' Chaunter ' and ' Drums ' ; but the Chaunter referred to is one of Edward Dorrit's creditors, and the word means ' not a singer of anthems, but a seller of horses.' To this profession also Simpson belonged, on whom Mr. Pickwick was ' chummed ' in the Fleet prison. A ' drum ' is referred to in the description of the London streets at night in *Barnaby Rudge*, and signifies a rout or evening party for cards ; while one where stakes ran high and much noise accompanied the play was known as a ' drum major.'

In *Our Bore* (R. P.) this sentence occurs :

He was at the Norwich musical festival when the extra-ordinary echo, for which science has been wholly unable to account, was heard for the first and last time. He and the bishop heard it at the same moment, and caught each other's eye.

Dr. A. H. Mann, who knows as much about Norwich and its festivals as any one, is quite unable to throw any light on this mystic remark. There were com-plaints about the acoustics of the St. Andrew's Hall many years ago, but there appears to be no historic foundation for Dickens' reference. It would certainly be interesting to know what suggested the idea to him.

There is a curious incident connected with Uncle Dick, whose great ambition was ' to beat the drum.' It was only by a mere chance that his celebrated reference to King Charles's head got into the story. Dickens originally wrote as follows (in Chapter 14, *D. C.*) :

' Do you recollect the date,' said Mr. Dick, looking earnestly at me, and taking up his pen to note it down, ' when the bull got into the china warehouse and did so much mischief ? '

In the proof Dickens struck out all the words after ' when,' and inserted in their place the following :

' King Charles the First had his head cut off ? '
I said I believed it happened in the year sixteen hundred and forty-nine.
' Well,' returned Mr. Dick, scratching his ear with his pen and looking dubiously at me, ' so the books say, but I don't see how that can be. Because if it was so long ago, how could the people about him have made that mistake of putting some of the trouble out of his head, after it was taken off, into mine ? '

The whole of the substituted passage is inserted in the margin at the bottom of the page. Again, when Mr. Dick shows David Copperfield his kite covered with manuscript, David was made to say in the proof : ' I thought I saw some allusion to the bull again in one or two places.'   Here Dickens has struck through the words, ' the bull,' and replaced them with ' King Charles the First's head.'

The original reference was to a very popular song of the period called ' The Bull in the China Shop,' words by C. Dibdin, Junior, and music by W. Reeve. Produced about 1808, it was popularized by the celebrated clown Grimaldi. The first verse is :

> You've heard of a frog in an opera hat,
> 'Tis a very old tale of a mouse and a rat,
> I could sing you another as pleasant, mayhap,
> Of a kitten that wore a high caul cap ;
> But my muse on a far nobler subject shall drop,
> Of a bull who got into a china shop,
>> With his right leg, left leg, upper leg, under leg,
>> St. Patrick's day in the morning.

CHAPTER VII

SOME NOTED SINGERS

The Micawbers

DICKENS presents us with such an array of characters who reckon singing amongst their various accomplishments that it is difficult to know where to begin. Perhaps the marvellous talents of the Micawber family entitle them to first place. Mrs. Micawber was famous for her interpretation of ' The Dashing White Sergeant ' and ' Little Taffline ' when she lived at home with her papa and mamma, and it was her rendering of these songs that gained her a spouse, for, as Mr. Micawber told Copperfield,

when he heard her sing the first one, on the first occasion of his seeing her beneath the parental roof, she had attracted his attention in an extraordinary degree, but that when it came to ' Little Tafflin,' he had resolved to win that woman or perish in the attempt.

It will be remembered that Mr. Bucket (*B. H.*) gained a wife by a similar display of vocal talent. After singing ' Believe me, if all those endearing

young charms,' he informs his friend Mrs. Bagnet
that this ballad was

his most powerful ally in moving the heart of Mrs. Bucket when
a maiden, and inducing her to approach the altar. Mr. Bucket's
own words are ' to come up to the scratch.'

Mrs. Micawber's ' Little Taffline ' was a song
in Storace's ballad opera *Three and the Deuce,*
words by Prince Hoare. It will be interesting
to see what the song which helped to mould
Micawber's fate was like.

LITTLE TAFFLINE.

Should e'er the for - tune be my lot To be
made a wealth - y bride, I'll glad my par - ents'
low - ly cot, All their plea - sure and their pride: And
when I'm drest all in my best, I'll trip a - way like
la - dy gay, I'll trip, I'll trip a - way. And the

lads will say,   Dear heart, what a flash! Look at little Taffline with a

silk-en sash, And the lads will say, Dear heart, what a flash! And the

lads will say, Dear heart, what a flash! Look at little Taffline, Look at

lit-tle Taf-fline, Oh, look at lit-tle Taffline with the silk-en sash!

There was also a character called Little Taffline in T. Dibdin's *St. David's Day*, the music for which was compiled and composed by Thomas Attwood, organist of St. Paul's Cathedral.

Her other song, 'The Dashing White Sergeant,' was a martial and very popular setting of some words by General Burgoyne.

Micawber could both sing and hum, and when music failed him he fell back on quotations. As he was subject to extremes of depression and elevation it was nothing unusual for him to commence a Saturday evening in tears and finish up with singing ' about Jack's delight being his lovely Nan ' towards the end of it. Here we gather that one of his favourite songs was C. Dibdin's ' Lovely Nan,' containing these two lines :

> But oh, much sweeter than all these
> Is Jack's delight, his lovely Nan.

His musical powers made him useful at the clubroom in the King's Bench, where David discovered him leading the chorus of ' Gee up, Dobbin.' This would be ' Mr. Doggett's Comicall Song ' in the farce *The Stage Coach*, containing the lines—

> With a hey gee up, gee up, hay ho ;
> With a hay gee, Dobbin, hey ho !

' Auld Lang Syne ' was another of Mr. Micawber's favourites, and when David joined the worthy pair in their lodgings at Canterbury they sang it with much energy. To use Micawber's words—

When we came to ' Here's a hand, my trusty frere ' we all joined hands round the table ; and when we declared we would ' take a right gude willie waught,' and hadn't the least idea what it meant, we were really affected.

The memory of this joyous evening recurred to Mr. M. at a later date, after the feast in David's rooms, and he calls to mind how they had sung

> We twa had run about the braes
> And pu'd the gowans fine.

I

He confesses his ignorance as to what gowans are,

but I have no doubt that Copperfield and myself would frequently have taken a pull at them, if it had been feasible.

In the last letter he writes he makes a further
quotation from the song. On another occasion,
however, under the stress of adverse circumstances
he finds consolation in a verse from ' Scots, wha
hae',' while at the end of the long epistle in which he
disclosed the infamy of Uriah Heep, he claims to
have it said of him, ' as of a gallant and eminent
naval Hero, that what he has done, he did

For England, home, and beauty.

' The Death of Nelson,' from which this line comes,
had a long run of popularity.   Braham, the composer, was one of the leading tenors of the day, and
thus had the advantage of being able to introduce
his own songs to the public.   The novelist's dictum
that ' composers can very seldom sing their own
music or anybody else's either' (*P. P.* 15) may be
true in the main, but scarcely applies to Braham,
who holds very high rank amongst English tenors.
Another song which he wrote with the title ' The
Victory and Death of Lord Viscount Nelson ' met
with no success.   The one quoted by Micawber

was naturally one of Captain Cuttle's favourites, and it is also made use of by Silas Wegg.

The musical gifts of Mr. and Mrs. Micawber descended to their son Wilkins, who had ' a remarkable head voice,' but having failed to get into the cathedral choir at Canterbury, he had to take to singing in public-houses instead of in sacred edifices. His great song appears to have been ' The Woodpecker Tapping.' When the family emigrated Mr. M. expressed the hope that ' the melody of my son will be acceptable at the galley fire ' on board ship. The final glimpse we get of him is at Port Middlebay, where he delights a large assembly by his rendering of ' Non Nobis ' (see p. 149), and by his dancing with the fourth daughter of Mr. Mell.

The ' Woodpecker ' song is referred to in an illustrative way by Mrs. Finching (*L. D.*), who says that her papa

is sitting prosily breaking his new-laid egg in the back parlour like the woodpecker tapping.

Captain Cuttle

Captain Cuttle is almost as full of melody as Micawber, though his repertoire is chiefly confined to naval ditties. His great song is ' Lovely Peg,'

and his admiration for Florence Dombey induces
him to substitute her name in the song, though the
best he can accomplish is ' Lovely Fleg.'

There are at least three eighteenth-century
ballads with Peg, or Lovely Peg, for the subject,
and it is not certain which of these the Captain
favoured.   This is one of them :

> Once more I'll tune the vocal shell,
> To Hills and Dales my passion tell,
> A flame which time can never quell,
> That burns for lovely Peggy.

Then comes this tuneful refrain :

Love - ly Peg-gy,   love - ly Peg-gy,   Love-ly, love-ly, love - ly Peg - gy; The heav'ns should sound with e - choes rung In praise of love - ly Peg - gy.

The two others of this period that I have seen are
called ' Peggy ' and ' Lovely Peggy, an imitation.'
However, it is most probable that the one that

the Captain favoured—in spite of the mixture of
names—was C. Dibdin's ' Lovely Polly.'

LOVELY POLLY

Dickens was very familiar with Dibdin's songs,
while the eighteenth-century ones referred to he

probably never heard of, as they are very rarely found.

The worthy Captain enjoys a good rollicking song, preferably of a patriotic turn, but is very unreliable as to the sources of his ditties.

> 'Wal'r, my boy,' replied the Captain, 'in the Proverbs of Solomon you will find the following words, "May we never want a friend in need, nor a bottle to give him!" When found, made a note of.'

This is taken from a song by J. Davy, known as 'Since the first dawn of reason,' and was sung by Incledon.

Since the first dawn of reason that beam'd on my mind,
  And taught me how favoured by fortune my lot,
To share that good fortune I still am inclined,
  And impart to who wanted what I wanted not.
It's a maxim entitled to every one's praise,
  When a man feels distress, like a man to relieve him;
And my motto, though simple, means more than it says,
  'May we ne'er want a friend or a bottle to give him.'

He is equally unreliable as to the source of a still more famous song. When Florence Dombey goes to see him the Captain intimates his intention of standing by old Sol Gills,

> 'and not desert until death do us part, and when the stormy winds do blow, do blow, do blow—overhaul the Catechism,' said

the Captain parenthetically, ' and there you'll find these ex-
pressions.'

I have not heard of any church that has found it
necessary to include this old refrain in its Catechism,
nor even to mix it up with the Wedding Service.

A further mixture of quotations occurs when he
is talking of Florence on another occasion. Speaking
of the supposed death of Walter he says,

> Though lost to sight, to memory dear, and
> England, home, and beauty.

The first part—which is one of Cuttle's favourite
quotations—is the first line of a song by G. Linley.
He composed a large number of operas and songs,
many of which were very popular. The second
part of the quotation is from Braham's ' Death of
Nelson ' (see p. 116).

In conversation with his friend Bunsby, Cuttle
says—

> Give me the lad with the tarry trousers as shines to me like
> di'monds bright, for which you'll overhaul the ' Stanfell's
> Budget,' and when found make a note.

Elsewhere he mentions Fairburn's ' Comic Songster '
and the ' Little Warbler ' as his song authorities.

The song referred to here is classed by Dr. Vaughan

Williams amongst Essex folk-songs, but it is by no means confined to that county. It tells of a mother who wants her daughter to marry a tailor, and not wait for her sailor bold.

> My mother wants me to wed with a tailor
> And not give me my heart's delight;
> But give me the man with the tarry trousers,
> That shines to me like diamonds bright.

After the firm of Dombey has decided to send Walter to Barbados, the boy discusses his prospects with his friend the Captain, and finally bursts into song—

How does that tune go that the sailors sing?

> For the port of Barbados, Boys!
> Cheerily!
> Leaving old England behind us, boys!
> Cheerily!

Here the Captain roared in chorus,

> Oh cheerily, cheerily!
> Oh cheer-i-ly!

All efforts to trace this song have failed, and for various reasons I am inclined to think that Dickens made up the lines to fit the occasion; while the words ' Oh cheerily, cheerily ' are a variant of a refrain common in sea songs, and the Captain teaches Rob the Grinder to sing it at a later period of the story. The arguments against the existence of such a song are: first, that the Dombey firm have already decided to send the boy to Barbados, and as there is no song suitable, the novelist invents one ; and in the second place there has never been a time in the history of Barbados to give rise to such a song as this, and no naval expedition of any consequence has ever been sent there. It is perhaps unnecessary to urge that there is no such place as the ' Port of Barbados.'

Dick Swiveller

None of Dickens' characters has such a wealth of poetical illustration at command as Mr. Richard Swiveller. He lights up the Brass office ' with scraps of song and merriment,' and when he is taking Kit's mother home in a depressed state after the trial he does his best to entertain her with ' astonishing absurdities in the way of quotation from song and poem.' From the time of his introduction, when he ' obliged the company with a few bars of an intensely dismal air,' to when he expresses his gratitude to the Marchioness—

> And she shall walk in silk attire,
> And siller have to spare—

there is scarcely a scene in which he is present when he does not illumine his remarks by quotations of some kind or other, though there are certainly a few occasions when his listeners are not always able to appreciate their aptness. For instance in the scene between Swiveller and the single gentleman, after the latter has been aroused from his slumbers, and has intimated he is not to be disturbed again.

' I beg your pardon,' said Dick, halting in his passage to the door, which the lodger prepared to open, ' when he who adores thee has left but the name——'

' What do you mean ? '

' But the name,' said Dick, ' has left but the name—in case of letters or parcels——'

' I never have any,' said the lodger.

' Or in case anybody should call.'

' Nobody ever calls on me.'

' If any mistake should arise from not having the name, don't say it was my fault, sir,' added Dick, still lingering ; ' oh, blame not the bard——'

' I'll blame nobody,' said the lodger.

But that Mr. Swiveller's knowledge of songs should be both ' extensive and peculiar ' is only to be expected from one who held the distinguished office of ' Perpetual Grand Master of the Glorious Apollers,' although he seems to have been more in the habit of quoting extracts from them than of giving vocal illustrations. On one occasion, however, we find him associated with Mr. Chuckster 'in a fragment of the popular duet of "All's Well" with a long shake at the end.'

The following extract illustrates the 'shake':

ALL'S WELL (Duet).

Sung by Mr. Braham and Mr. Charles Braham.

Music by Mr. Braham.

Although most of Swiveller's quotations are from songs, he does not always confine himself to them, as for instance, when he sticks his fork into a large carbuncular potato and reflects that 'Man wants but little here below,' which seems to show that in his quieter moments he had studied Goldsmith's *Hermit*.

Mr. Swiveller's quotations are largely connected with his love-passages with Sophy Wackles, and they are so carefully and delicately graded that they practically cover the whole ground in the rise and decline of his affections. He begins by suggesting that ' she's all my fancy painted her.'

From this he passes to

> She's like the red, red rose,
>   That's newly sprung in June.
> She's also like a melody,
>   That's sweetly played in tune.

then

> When the heart of a man is depressed with fears,
> The mist is dispelled when Miss Wackles appears,

which is his own variant of

> If the heart of a man is depressed with care,
> The mist is dispelled when a woman appears.

But at the party given by the Wackleses Dick finds he is cut out by Mr. Cheggs, and so makes his escape saying, as he goes—

> My boat is on the shore, and my bark is on the sea; but before I pass this door, I will say farewell to thee,

and he subsequently adds—

> Miss Wackles, I believed you true, and I was blessed in so believing; but now I mourn that e'er I knew a girl so fair, yet so deceiving.

The *dénouement* occurs some time after, when, in
the course of an interview with Quilp, he takes from
his pocket

a small and very greasy parcel, slowly unfolding it, and dis-
playing a little slab of plum cake, extremely indigestible in
appearance and bordered with a paste of sugar an inch and a
half deep.

'What should you say this was?' demanded Mr. Swiveller.

'It looks like bride-cake,' replied the dwarf, grinning.

'And whose should you say it was?' inquired Mr. Swiveller,
rubbing the pastry against his nose with dreadful calmness.
'Whose?'

'Not——'

'Yes,' said Dick, 'the same. You needn't mention her name.
There's no such name now. Her name is Cheggs now, Sophy
Cheggs. Yet loved I as man never loved that hadn't wooden
legs, and my heart, my heart is breaking for the love of Sophy
Cheggs.'

With this extemporary adaptation of a popular ballad to the
distressing circumstances of his own case, Mr. Swiveller folded
up the parcel again, beat it very flat upon the palms of his
hands, thrust it into his breast, buttoned his coat over it, and
folded his arms upon the whole.

And then he signifies his grief by pinning a piece of
crape on his hat, saying as he did so,

> 'Twas ever thus: from childhood's hour
> I've seen my fondest hopes decay;
> I never loved a tree or flower
> But 'twas the first to fade away;

> I never nursed a dear gazelle,
>   To glad me with its soft black eye,
> But when it came to know me well,
>   And love me, it was sure to marry a market
>   gardener.

He is full of song when entertaining the
Marchioness. ' Do they often go where glory waits
'em ? ' he asks, on hearing that Sampson and Sally
Brass have gone out for the evening. He accepts
the statement that Miss Brass thinks him a ' funny
chap ' by affirming that ' Old King Cole was a merry
old soul ' ; and on taking his leave of the little
slavey he says,

' Good night, Marchioness. Fare thee well, and if for ever
then for ever fare thee well—and put up the chain, Marchioness,
in case of accidents.

> Since life like a river is flowing,
>   I care not how fast it rolls on, ma'am,
> While such purl on the bank still is growing,
>   And such eyes light the waves as they run.'

On a later occasion, after enjoying some games
of cards he retires to rest in a deeply contemplative
mood.

' These rubbers,' said Mr. Swiveller, putting on his nightcap
in exactly the same style as he wore his hat, ' remind me of
the matrimonial fireside. Cheggs's wife plays cribbage ; all-
fours likewise. She rings the changes on 'em now. From sport

to sport they hurry her, to banish her regrets ; and when they win a smile from her they think that she forgets—but she don't.'

Many of Mr. Swiveller's quotations are from Moore's *Irish Melodies*, though he has certainly omitted one which, coming from him, would not have been out of place, viz. ' The time I've lost in wooing ' !

On another occasion Swiveller recalls some well-known lines when talking to Kit. ' An excellent woman, that mother of yours, Christopher,' said Mr. Swiveller ; ' " Who ran to catch me when I fell, and kissed the place to make it well ? My mother." '

This is from Ann Taylor's nursery song, which has probably been more parodied than any other poem in existence. There is a French version by Madame à Taslie, and it has most likely been translated into other languages.

Dick gives us another touching reference to his mother. He is overcome with curiosity to know in what part of the Brass establishment the Marchioness has her abode.

My mother must have been a very inquisitive woman ; I have no doubt I'm marked with a note of interrogation somewhere. My feelings I smother, but thou hast been the cause of this anguish, my——

This last remark is a memory of T. H. Bayly's
celebrated song ' We met,' which tells in somewhat
incoherent language the story of a maiden who left
her true love at the command of her mother, and
married for money.

> The world may think me gay,
>   For my feelings I smother;
> Oh *thou* hast been the cause
>   Of this anguish—my mother.

T. Haynes Bayly was a prominent song-writer
some seventy years ago (1797–1839). His most
popular ballad was ' I'd be a Butterfly.' It came
out with a coloured title-page, and at once became
the rage, in fact, as John Hullah said, ' half musical
England was smitten with an overpowering, resist-
less rage for metempsychosis.' There were many
imitations, such as ' I'd be a Nightingale ' and
' I'd be an Antelope.'

Teachers and Composers

Although we read so much about singers, the
singing-master is rarely introduced, in fact Mr.
M'Choakumchild (*H. T.*), who ' could teach every-
thing from vocal music to general cosmography,'
almost stands alone. However, in view of the

complaints of certain adjudicators about the facial distortions they beheld at musical competitions, it may be well to record Mrs. General's recipe for giving ' a pretty form to the lips ' (*L. D.*).

Papa, potatoes, poultry, prunes, and prism are all very good words for the lips, especially prunes and prism. You will find it serviceable in the formation of a demeanour.

Nor do composers receive much attention, but amongst the characters we may mention Mr. Skimpole (*B. H.*), who composed half an opera, and the lamp porter at Mugby Junction, who composed ' Little comic songs-like.' In this category we can scarcely include Mrs. Kenwigs, who ' invented and composed ' her eldest daughter's name, the result being ' Morleena.' Mr. Skimpole, however, has a further claim upon our attention, as he ' played what he composed with taste,' and was also a performer on the violoncello. He had his lighter moments, too, as when he went to the piano one evening at 11 p.m. and rattled hilariously

That the best of all ways to lengthen our days
Was to steal a few hours from Night, my dear !

It is evident that his song was ' The Young May Moon,' one of Moore's *Irish Melodies.*

K

The young May moon is beaming, love,
The glow-worm's lamp is gleaming, love,
How sweet to rove
Through Morna's grove
While the drowsy world is dreaming, love !

Then awake—the heavens look bright, my dear !
'Tis never too late for delight, my dear !
And the best of all ways
To lengthen our days
Is to steal a few hours from the night, my dear !

Silas Wegg's Effusions

We first meet Silas Wegg in the fifth chapter of *Our Mutual Friend*, where he is introduced to us as a ballad-monger. His intercourse with his employer, Mr. Boffin, is a frequent cause of his dropping into poetry, and most of his efforts are adaptations of popular songs. His character is not one that arouses any sympathetic enthusiasm, and probably no one is sorry when towards the end of the story Sloppy seizes hold of the mean little creature, carries him out of the house, and deposits him in a scavenger's cart 'with a prodigious splash.'

The following are Wegg's poetical effusions, with their sources and original forms.

Book I, Ch. 5.   ' Beside that cottage door, Mr. Boffin,' from
  ' The Soldier's Tear '   *Alexander Lee*

> Beside that cottage porch
> A girl was on her knees ;
> She held aloft a snowy scarf
> Which fluttered in the breeze.
> She breath'd a prayer for him,
> A prayer he could not hear ;
> But he paused to bless her as she knelt,
> And wip'd away a tear.

Book I, Ch. 15.

> The gay, the gay and festive scene,
> I'll tell thee how the maiden wept, Mrs. Boffin.

From ' The Light Guitar.'   (See Index of Songs.)

Book I, Ch. 15.   ' Thrown on the wide world, doomed to
  wander and roam.' From ' The Peasant Boy '   *J. Parry*

> Thrown on the wide world, doom'd to wander and roam,
> Bereft of his parents, bereft of his home,
> A stranger to pleasure, to comfort and joy,
> Behold little Edmund, the poor Peasant Boy.

Book I, Ch. 15.   ' Weep for the hour.'   From ' Eveleen's
  Bower '   *T. Moore*

> Oh ! weep for the hour
> When to Eveleen's bower
> The lord of the valley with false vows came.

Book I, Ch 15.   ' Then farewell, my trim-built wherry.'   From
  ' The Waterman '   *C. Dibdin*

Book II, Ch. 7.   ' Helm a-weather, now lay her close.'   From
  ' The Tar for all Weathers '   *Unknown*

Book III, Ch. 6.   ' No malice to dread, sir.'   From verse 3 of
'My Ain Fireside.'   Words by *Mrs. E. Hamilton*

> Nae falsehood to dread, nae malice to fear,
> But truth to delight me, and kindness to cheer;
> O' a' roads to pleasure that ever were tried,
> There's nane half so sure as one's own fireside.
>> My ain fireside, my ain fireside,
>> Oh sweet is the blink o' my ain fireside.

Book III, Ch. 6.

> And you needn't, Mr. Venus, be your black bottle,
>> For surely I'll be mine,
> And we'll take a glass with a slice of lemon in it, to
>> which you're partial,
>> For auld lang syne.

A much altered version of verse 5 of Burns' celebrated
song.

Book III, Ch. 6.

>> Charge, Chester, charge,
>> On Mr. Venus, on.

From Scott's *Marmion.*

Book IV, Ch. 3.   ' If you'll come to the bower I've shaded for
you.'   From ' Will you Come to the Bower '   *T. Moore*

> Will you come to the Bower I've shaded for you,
> Our bed shall be roses, all spangled with dew.
> Will you, will you, will you, will you come to the Bower?
> Will you, will you, will you, will you come to the Bower?

A LIST OF SONGS

INSTRUMENTAL MUSIC MENTIONED BY DICKENS

WITH HISTORICAL NOTES

The figures in brackets denote the chapter in the novel referred to

A COBBLER THERE WAS (*D. & S.* 2)

> A cobbler there was, and he lived in a stall,
> Which serv'd him for parlour, for kitchen and hall,
> No coin in his pocket, nor care in his pate,
> No ambition had he, nor no duns at his gate.
> > Derry down, down, down, derry down.

The melody appeared in *Beggar's Opera*, 1728, and *Fashionable Lady*, 1730.

A FROG HE WOULD (*P.P.* 32)

The theme of the ballad belongs to the late sixteenth century.

> A frog he would a-wooing go,
> > Heigho! said Rowley,
> Whether his mother would let him or no,
> > With his rowly powly,
> > Gammon and spinnage,
> > > O heigh! said Anthony Rowley.

We are told that Jack Hopkins sang 'The King, God Bless Him,' to a novel air, compounded of 'The Bay of Biscay' and 'A Frog He Would.' The latter was evidently the modern setting by C. E. Horn.

ALICE GRAY

See 'Yet Lov'd I.'

ALL HAIL TO THE VESSEL OF PECKSNIFF THE SIRE (*M.C.* 11)

Perhaps a parody on 'All Hail to the Chief.'

ALL IN THE DOWNS (*P.P.* 3)

See 'Black-Eyed Susan.'

ALL'S WELL (*O.C.S.* 56).   See p. 125.

Duet in *The English Fleet.*

(*T. Dibdin*)   *J. Braham.*

> Deserted by the waning moon,
> When skies proclaim night's cheerless gloom,
> On tower, fort, or tented ground,
> The sentry walks his lonely round ;
> And should a footstep haply stray
> Where caution marks the guarded way,
> Who goes there ? Stranger, quickly tell,
> A friend. The word ? Good-night. All's well.

AND SHE SHALL WALK (*O.C.S.* 66)

Words by *Susan Blamire.*

> And ye shall walk in silk attire,
>   And siller ha'e to spare,
> Gin ye'll consent to be my bride,
>   Nor think on Donald mair.

Susan Blamire was born at Carden Hall, near Carlisle.
Very few of her poems were published under her own
name, as well-born ladies of those days disliked seeing
their names published as authors. ' The Siller Crown,'
from which this verse is taken, is in the Cumberland
dialect. It first appeared anonymously in the *Scots
Musical Museum,* 1790, and the authorship was subsequently settled by members of the family.

AND YOU NEEDN'T, MR. VENUS, BE YOUR BLACK BOTTLE
(*O.M.F.*).   See p. 134.

A STIFF NOR'-WESTER'S BLOWING, BILL (*D. & S.* 49)

From ' The Sailor's Consolation.'

> One night came on a hurricane,
>   The seas were mountains rolling,
> When Barney Buntline turned his quid,
>   And said to Billy Bowling,
> A stiff Nor'-Wester's blowing, Bill,
>   Hark, don't you hear it roar now?
> Lord help 'em ! how I pity's all
>   Unhappy folk ashore now.

Mr. Kidson says in reference to this : ' I do not know that it was ever written to music, though I fancy more than one popular tune has been set to the words, which are by a person named Pitt.'

AULD LANG SYNE (' Holly Tree,' *D.C.* 17, 28)

Words by *Burns.*

A version of the melody occurs at the end of the overture to Shield's *Rosina*, 1783, and is either his own composition or an imitation of some Scotch melody. As, however, such melody has not hitherto been discovered, no great importance can be attached to this theory. *Rosina* was performed in Edinburgh.

Some maintain that the tune is taken from a Scotch reel known as the ' Miller's Wedding,' found in Bremner's *Reels* (1757–1761).

AWAY WITH MELANCHOLY (*O.C.S.* 58, *O.M.F.* ii. 6, *P.P.* 44, *D.C.* 8)

The melody is from Mozart's *Magic Flute*, ' Das klinget so herrlich '—a chorus with glockenspiel accompaniment. The writer of the words is unknown.

The air was introduced into an arrangement of Shakespeare's *Tempest*, and set to the words ' To moments so delighting ! ' sung by Miss Stephens. Also found as a duet ' composed by Sigr. Mozart, arranged by F. A. Hyde.'

BAY OF BISCAY (*U.T.* 31, *D. & S.* 39, *P.P.* 32)

Words by *Andrew Cherry*.   *J. Davy.*

Also see under ' A Frog He Would.'

BEETHOVEN'S SONATA IN B. See p. 28.

BEGONE, DULL CARE (*O.C.S.* 7, *E.D.* 2)

> Author unknown. The words occur in various song-books of the eighteenth century. The tune is seventeenth century, possibly derived from the 'Queen's Jigg' in the *Dancing Master*.
>
>> Begone, dull care, I prithee begone from me;
>> Begone, dull care, you and I can never agree.
>
> The words were set as a glee by John Sale, and this may be the music that Dickens knew.

BELIEVE ME, IF ALL JARLEY'S WAXWORKS SO RARE (*O.C.S.* 27)

> A parody on the following.

BELIEVE ME, IF ALL THOSE ENDEARING YOUNG CHARMS (*B.H.* 55)

> Words by *T. Moore*.
>
> Set to the old melody 'My Lodging is on the Cold Ground.' This appears to have come into existence about the middle of the eighteenth century. It is found in *Vocal Music, or the Songster's Companion*, 1775, and it was claimed by Moore to be an Irish melody, but some authorities deny this. It has also been claimed as Scotch, but the balance of opinion is in favour of its English origin (F. Kidson).

BESIDE THAT COTTAGE DOOR, MR. BOFFIN (*O.M.F.*)

> See p. 133.

BID ME DISCOURSE (*S.B.T.* 4)

> Words adapted from Shakespeare's *Venus and Adonis*.
>   *H. R. Bishop.*

BIRD WALTZ (*D. & S.* 29, 38)   *Panormo.*

> A very popular piano piece of the pre-Victorian period.

BLACK-EYED SUSAN *(A.N.)*, OR ALL IN THE DOWNS *(P.P. 3)*

Words by *John Gay.* R. *Leveridge.*

This song was printed in sheet form previous to 1730, in which year it appeared in Watts' *Musical Miscellany,* Vol. IV., and was also inserted about that time in several ballad operas.

BOLD TURPIN VUNCE *(P.P. 43)*

Mr. Frank Kidson has pointed out that Sam Weller's song is founded upon a ballad entitled ' Turpin and the Bishop,' which appears in *Gaieties and Gravities,* by one of the authors of *Rejected Addresses.* The author is said to be Horatio Smith. There is a good four-part setting of the words by Sir F. Bridge.

BRAVE LODGINGS FOR ONE *(P.P. 29)*

Original.

BRITISH GRENADIERS *(B.H. 49)*

The tune as we know it now is the growth of centuries, the foundation probably being a tune in *The Fitzwilliam Virginal Book.* The Grenadiers were founded in 1678. The second verse refers to ' hand grenades,' and the regiment ceased to use these in the reign of Queen Anne. The author is unknown.

BRITONS, STRIKE HOME *(S.L.)*

The well-known song in Purcell's *Bonduca* gave its name to an opera by Charles Dibdin, published in 1803. This work probably suggested the phrase to Dickens. It was written with a view to arousing a patriotic feeling.

The following verse occurs in the work :

> When Dryden wrote and Purcell sung
> Britons, strike home,
> The patriot-sounds re-echoing rung
> The vaulted dome.

BUFFALO GALS (*Letters*)

See p. 10.

BY THE SAD SEA WAVES (*Letters*)   *Julius Benedict.*

A once popular song from the opera *The Brides of Venice.*

CHEER, BOYS, CHEER (*U.T.* 29)

Words by *Charles Mackay.*   *Henry Russell.*

> Cheer ! boys, cheer ! no more of idle sorrow—
> Courage ! true hearts shall bear us on our way,
> Hope points before, and shows the bright to-morrow,
> Let us forget the darkness of to-day.

One of Russell's most popular songs. He sold the copyright for £3, and shortly afterwards learnt that the publisher had to keep thirty-nine presses at work on it night and day to meet the demand.

COPENHAGEN WALTZ (*D. & S.* 7)

Also known as the *Danish Waltz.*

DEAD MARCH.

From the oratorio *Saul.*   *Handel.*

See p. 61.

DEATH OF NELSON (*D.C.* 52, *D. & S.* 48, *O.M.F.* iv. 3)

See p. 116.   *J. Braham.*

> Too well the gallant hero fought,
> For England, home, and beauty.

DI PIACER (*S.B.T.* 1) *Rossini.*

A favourite air from the opera *La Gazza Ladra.*

DOWNFALL OF PARIS

See p. 31.

DRAGON OF WANTLEY (*D.C.* 38)

An eighteenth-century popular burlesque opera.
Words by *H. Carey*, music by *Lampe.*

DRINK TO ME ONLY WITH THINE EYES (*O.M.F.* iii. 14)

Words by *Ben Jonson.*

The composer is unknown. The air was originally
issued as a glee for three voices.

DUMBLEDUMDEARY (*S.B. S.* 10)

A refrain rarely found in old songs. It occurs in
' Richard of Taunton Dean.' Also (as in the reference)
the name of a dance.

EVENING BELLS (*D.C.* 38)

Duet by *G. Alexander Lee.*
Come away, come away, evening bells are ringing,
Sweetly, sweetly ; 'tis the vesper hour.

FARE THEE WELL, AND IF FOR EVER (*O.C.S.* 58)

Words by *Byron.*

Included in ' Domestic Pieces.'

Fare thee well, and if for ever,
Still for ever, fare thee well ;
Even though unforgiving, never
'Gainst thee shall my heart rebel.

About 1825 the words were set to an air from Mozart's
La Clemenza di Tito. There are original settings by
Parke, S. Webbe, and six other composers.

FILL THE BUMPER FAIR (*N. T.*)

Moore's *Irish Melodies*, air ' Bob and Joan.'

FLOW ON, THOU SHINING RIVER (*S.B.T.* 1)

Moore's *National Melodies.*

Said to be a ' Portuguese Air.' The melody has been utilized as a hymn-tune.

FLY, FLY FROM THE WORLD, MY BESSY, WITH ME (*S.B. S.* 2)

Words and music by *T. Moore.*

FOR ENGLAND

See ' Death of Nelson.'

FOR ENGLAND, HOME, AND BEAUTY

See ' Death of Nelson.'

FOR THE PORT OF BARBADOS, BOYS (*D. & S.* 15)

Original (?) See p. 122.

FROM SPORT TO SPORT (*O.C.S.* 58)

From ' Oh no, we never mention her.'

Words by *T. H. Bayly.*   *H. R. Bishop.*

From sport to sport they hurry me,
  To banish my regret ;
And when they win a smile from me,
  They think that I forget.

GEE UP, DOBBIN (*D.C.* 12)

In the Burney Collection is a tune ' Gee Ho, Dobbin.' Also in *Apollo's Cabinet*, 1757, Vol. II, and *Love in a*

Village, 1762. The tune was frequently used for ephemeral songs.

It is doubtful if Dickens would know this song, the title of which has passed into a common phrase.

GLORIOUS APOLLO (*O.C.S.* 13, 56)   *S. Webbe.*

The title of this glee probably suggested the name of the ' Glorious Apollers.' See p. 124.

GO WHERE GLORY WAITS THEE (*M.C.* 11)

(' Do they often go where glory waits 'em ? ' *O.C.S.* 58) Moore's *Irish Melodies,* set to the air ' Maid of the Valley.'

GOD BLESS THE PRINCE OF WALES (*U.T.* 29)

Words by *J. Ceiriog Hughes.*   *H. Brinley Richards,* Trans. by G. Linley.   1862.

GOD BLESS YOU, MERRY GENTLEMEN (*C.C.*)

Origin unknown. The second word should be ' rest,' and the correct reading is

God rest you merry, gentlemen.

GOD SAVE THE KING (*S.B.S.* 19, &c.)

GOD SAVE THE QUEEN (*M.C.* 29)

It is unnecessary here to discuss the origin and sources of this air. The form in which we know it is probably due to Henry Carey, and the first recorded public performance was on September 28, 1745.

HAD I A HEART FOR FALSEHOOD FRAMED (*D. & S.* 14)

Words by *R. B. Sheridan.*

Sung by Mr. Leoni (see *Choir*, May, 1912).

In the *Duenna*, 1775. Set to the air now known as ' The Harp that once through Tara's Halls.'

Moore, in his *Irish Melodies*, calls the melody ' Gramachree.'

HAIL COLUMBIA (*M.C.* 13, *A.N.*)

Mr. Elson (*National Music of America*) says that the music was originally known as the ' President's March,' probably by a German composer. The words were subsequently adapted to the air by Dr. Joseph Hopkinson.

HARMONIOUS BLACKSMITH (*G.E.* 21)

From Handel's *Suite de Pièces pour le Clavecin*, Set I. See p. 19.

HAS SHE THEN FAILED IN HER TRUTH (*N. N.* 49)

Anon.   *H. R. Bishop.*

> And has she then failed in her truth,
>   The beautiful maid I adore ?
> Shall I never again hear her voice,
>   Nor see her lov'd form any more ?

HEART OF OAK (*B.R.* 7, *E.D.* 12, *U.T.* 20, parody)

Words by *D. Garrick.*   *W. Boyce.*

It is important to notice that the correct title is as given, and not ' *Hearts* of Oak.'

HELM A WEATHER, NOW LAY HER CLOSE (*O.M.F.*)

See p. 133.

How Doth the Little———— (*Ch.*)   *Dr. Watts.*
See p. 79.

I am a Friar of Orders Grey (*S.B.S.* 8) (*Out of Season*)
Words by *John O'Keefe.*   *Wm. Reeve.*
Appeared in *Merry Sherwood*, 1795.

I Care Not For Spring
See p. 99.

I'd Crowns Resign, To Call Her Mine (*D.C.* 25)

'Lass of Richmond Hill.'

Words by *L. MacNally.*   *J. Hook.*

> I'd crowns resign, to call her mine,
> Sweet lass of Richmond Hill.

For a long time there was a dispute between the partisans of Surrey and Yorkshire as to which 'Richmond Hill' was referred to. The former county was the favourite for a long time, till a communication in *Notes and Queries* (10th series iii. p. 290) pulverized its hopes and definitely placed the locality in Yorkshire.

If I Had a Donkey (*O.C.S.* 27)
See p. 95.

If You'll Come to the Bower (*O.M.F.*)
See p. 134.

I'll Tell Thee How the Maiden Wept (*O.M.F.*)
See p. 133.

In Hurry, Post Haste for a Licence (*P.P.* 10)
See p. 90.

I Saw Her at the Fancy Fair (*S.B.T.* 11)

I Saw Thy Show in Youthful Prime (*D.C.S.* 27)

Moore's *Irish Melodies*, air ' Domhnall.'

> I saw thy form in youthful prime,
>   Nor thought that pale decay
> Would steal before the steps of time,
>   And waste its bloom away, Mary.

Isle of the Brave and Land of the Free (*M.J.*)
Original.

It May Lighten and Storm (*M.C.* 42)

Possibly from some old ballad opera, but more probably original.

Jack's Delight (to) His Lovely Nan (*D.C.* 11)

Words and music by *C. Dibdin.*

From ' Lovely Nan.' Last two lines :

> But oh, much sweeter than all these,
> Is Jack's delight, his lovely Nan.

Jim Crow (*A.N.*)   *Unknown.*

See p. 97.

> I come from old Kentucky,
>   A long time ago,
> Where I first larn to wheel about,
>   And jump Jim Crow ;
> Wheel about and turn about,
>   And do jis so,
> Eb'ry time I wheel about,
>   I jump Jim Crow.

Jolly Young Waterman (*It., P.P.* 33)
Words and music by *C. Dibdin* in *The Waterman.*

King Death (*B.H.* 33)

Words by *Barry Cornwall.* *Neukomm.*

> King Death was a rare old fellow,
> He sat where no sun could shine,
> And he lifted his hand so yellow,
> And pour'd out his coal-black wine.
> Hurrah for the coal-black wine !

John Leech used to sing ' King Death,' and it was of his voice that Jerrold once remarked, ' I say, Leech, if you had the same opportunity of exercising your voice as you have of using your pencil, how it would *draw* ! '

Lesbia Hath a Beaming Eye (*Letter to Lemon*)

Words by *Moore.*

Set to the delightfully gay air ' Nora Creina.'

> Lesbia hath a beaming eye,
> But no one knows for whom it beameth,
> Right and left its arrows fly,
> But what they aim at no one dreameth !

Listen to the Waterfall (*B.H.* 32)

Lord Mornington.

From the glee ' Here in cool grot.'

Little Taffline (*D.C.* 28)

Words by *Prince Hoare.* *S. Storace.*

In the opera *Three and The Deuce*, produced in 1806. See pp. 112, 113.

There is a character ' Little Taffline ' in T. Dibdin's *St. David's Day*, music composed and compiled by Attwood. There is another setting said to be ' composed by J. Parry,' but it is merely an altered form of the original.

L

LOVELY PEG (*D. & S.* 10)

See pp. 117-119.

MARSEILLAISE (*M.C.* 15, *E.D.* 2, *L.D.* 2)

Rouget de Lisle.

For brief history see *The Choir* (Nov., 1911)

MASANIELLO (*S.B.T.* 9)

Opera by *Auber.*
See p. 26.

MAY WE NE'ER WANT A FRIEND (*D. & S.* 15)

See 'When the first dawn of reason.'

MEN OF PROMETHEUS (*S.B.T.* 9)

See p. 26.

This was the name given to the first edition of Beethoven's ballet music to *Prometheus*, composed in 1800.

MISS WACKLES, I BELIEVED YOU TRUE (*O.C.S.* 8)

'Mary, I believed thee true,' *Moore* (one of his 'Juvenile Poems').

> Mary, I believed thee true,
>   And I was blest in so believing,
> But now I mourn that e'er I knew
>   A girl so fair and so deceiving!

It has been suggested that these words were adapted and sung to the Scotch air 'Gala Water.'

MY BOAT IS ON THE SHORE (*G.S.*) (*D.C.* 54, *Letters*)

Words by *Lord Byron.*   *Bishop.*
See p. 12.
Also set by W. Cratherne.

My Feelings I Smother (*O.C.S.* 36)
See ' We met.'

My Heart's in the Highlands (*O.C.S.* 2, *S.B.S.* 2)
Words partly by *Burns.*
In Captain Fraser's *Airs Peculiar to the Scottish Highlands,* 1816.
There is a parody by Dickens (see Forster's *Life,* ch. 8).

Never Leave off Dancing (*D.C.* 41)
Said to be the subject of a French song.

No Malice to Dread, Sir (*O.M.F.*)
See p. 134.

Non Nobis (*S.B.S.* 19)
This celebrated canon, by Byrd, has been performed at public dinners from time immemorial. It also used to be performed at the Theatre Royal, Covent Garden.

Now's the Day, and Now's the Hour (*D.C.* 54)
Verse 2 of ' Scots, Wha Hae ' (*Burns*).

> Now's the day, and now's the hour,
> See the front o' battle lour,
> See approach proud Edward's power,
> Chains and slaverie.

Of All the Girls That Are so Smart (*O.C.S.* 50)
Words and music by *Henry Carey.*

Carey composed his melody in 1715. It soon became popular, but owing to the similarity of certain phrases to those of an older tune known as ' The Country Lass,' the two gradually got mixed up, with the result that the latter became the recognized setting.

OFF SHE GOES (*S.B.T.* 7)

A once popular dance air.

OFT IN THE STILLY NIGHT (*S.B.S.* 13)

From T. Moore's *National Airs*, set to an air possibly of Scotch origin.   There are also settings by Stevenson and Hullah.

OH BLAME NOT THE BARD (*O.C.S.* 35)

Words by *T. Moore.*

In *Irish Melodies.*   Set to the tune ' Kitty Tyrrel.'

OH GIVE ME BUT MY ARAB STEED (*O.C.S.* 21)

Words by *T. H. Bayly.*   *G. A. Hodson.*

Written in 1828.   Sung by Braham.

> Oh give me but my Arab steed,
> My prince defends his right,
> And I will to the battle speed,
> To guard him in the fight.

OH CHEERILY, CHEERILY (*D. & S.* 32)

Original, but a refrain similar to this is not uncommon in old sea songs.

OH LADY FAIR (*G.E.* 13)

Trio by *Moore.*

See ' Strew then, O strew.'

OH LET US LOVE OUR OCCUPATIONS (*Ch.*)

Original lines by Dickens.   ' Set to music on the new system,' probably refers to Hullah's method (c. 1841), or possibly the Tonic Sol-fa (c. 1843), see p. 17.

OH LANDSMEN ARE FOLLY (*H.R.*)
    Original.

OLD CLEM (*G.E.* 12, 15)

A custom prevailed at Chatham of holding a procession on St. Clement's day, and the saint, who was irreverently designated 'Old Clem,' was personated by a young smith disguised for the occasion.

Dickens frequently writes a verse in the form of prose, and this is an example. Written out properly, it reads thus :

> Hammer boys round—Old Clem,
> With a thump and a sound—Old Clem,
> Beat it out, beat it out—Old Clem,
> With a cluck for the stout—Old Clem,
> Blow the fire, blow the fire—Old Clem,
> Roaring drier, soaring higher—Old Clem.

OLD KING COLE (*O.C.S.* 58, *P.P.* 36)

The personality of this gentleman has never been settled. Chappell suggests he was 'Old Cole,' a cloth-maker of Reading *temp.* Henry I. Wardle's carol 'I care not for spring' (*P.P.* 36) was adapted to this air, and printed in How's *Illustrated Book of British Song*.

OVER THE HILLS AND FAR AWAY (*Dr. M., M.C.* 36)

An old saying, both in song and as a phrase. It occurs in two songs in D'Urfey's *Pills to Purge Melancholy*, 1709, one of which is,

> Tom he was a piper's son,
> He learned to play when he was young ;
> But all the tune that he could play
> Was over the hills and far away.   (Vol. iv.)

Doctor Marigold's version is probably original :

> North and South and West and East,
> Winds liked best and winds liked least,
> Here and there and gone astray,
> Over the hills and far away.

OVER THE WATER TO CHARLIE (*O.C.S.* 27)

Tune in Johnson's *Musical Museum*, Vol. II, 1788.

> Come boat me o'er, come row me o'er,
>   Come boat me o'er to Charlie,
> I'll gie John Brown another half-crown,
>   To boat me o'er to Charlie ;
> We'll o'er the water, we'll o'er the sea,
>   We'll o'er the water to Charlie,
> Come weal, come woe, we'll gather and go,
>   And live or die wi' Charlie.

Another Jacobite song was the cause of an amusing incident at Edinburgh. On the occasion of one of his visits there Dickens went to the theatre, and he and his friends were much amazed and amused by the orchestra playing ' Charlie is my darling ' amid tumultuous shouts of delight.

PAUL AND VIRGINIA (*S.B.T.* 7, *L.D.* 13)

J. Mazzinghi.

The popular duet from this opera ' See from ocean rising ' was sung by Mr. Johnstone and Mr. Incledon. See p. 91.

POLLY PUT THE KETTLE ON (*B.R.* 24)

An old country dance.

RED RUFFIAN, RETIRE ! (*S.B.C.* 8)

Probably an imaginary title, invented by Dickens.

Rule Britannia (*D. & S.* 4, 39, *U.T.* 2, *M.C.* 11, 17, *A.N.*, *D.C.* 8)

> Words by *Thomson* or *Mallet.*   *Arne.*
>
> First appeared in print at the end of the masque *The Judgement of Paris*, but it was composed for the masque of *Alfred*, which was first performed on August 1, 1740. See *Musical Times*, April, 1900.

Sally in Our Alley

> See ' Of all the girls.'

Satan Finds Some Mischief Still (*D.C.* 16)

> See p. 80.   *Dr. Watts.*

See from Ocean Rising (*S.B.T.* 7)

> See *Paul and Virginia.*

She's All My Fancy Painted Her (*O.C.S.* 7)

> (' Alice Gray.')
> See ' Yet lov'd I.'

She's Like the Red, Red Rose (*O.C.S.* 8)

> Burns revised the words from an old song.
> The music is in *Caledonian Pocket Companion*, Bk. VII, 1754, under the name ' Low Down in the Broom.'

Shivery Shakey, Ain't It Cold (*Dr. M.*)

> See p. 94.

Since Laws Were Made for Every Degree (*O.C.S.* 66, *L.D.* ii. 12)

> Tyburn Tree.
>
> Since laws were made for ev'ry degree
> To curb vice in others as well as me,
> I wonder we han't better company
> Upon Tyburn Tree.
>
> From *Beggar's Opera.* Words by *Gay.*

Set to the tune of ' Greensleeves,' which dates from 1580. This tune is twice mentioned by Shakespeare in *The Merry Wives of Windsor.* An earlier ' Tyburn ' version is a song entitled ' A Warning to False Traitors,' which refers to the execution of six people at ' Tyborne ' on August 30, 1588.

SINCE THE FIRST DAWN OF REASON   *J. Davy.*

See p. 120.

SONG ABOUT A SPARKLING BOWL (*Ch.*)

There are several songs of this nature, such as ' The Flowing Bowl ' (' Fill the bowl with sparkling nectar '). Another began ' Fill, fill the bowl with sparkling wine.'

SONG ABOUT THE SLUMBERING ECHOES IN THE CAVERN OF MEMORY (*D.C.* 33)

Not at present traced.

STREW THEN, OH STREW A BED OF RUSHES (*O.C.S.* 65)

Words and music by *Moore.*

From the glee ' Holy be the Pilgrim's Sleep,' which is a sequel to ' Oh Lady Fair ' (q.v.).

Moore wrote two inane songs, entitled ' Holy be the Pilgrim's Sleep ' and ' Oh Lady Fair.' For both pilgrim and lady arrangements are made for spending the night somewhere, and in each song occur the words

Strew then, oh strew his [our] bed of rushes,
Here he shall [we must] rest till morning blushes.

TAMAROO (*M.C.* 32)

Said to be taken from an English ballad in which it is supposed to express the bold and fiery nature of a certain hackney coachman.

According to *Notes and Queries* (x. 1), this was sung at Winchester School some seventy or eighty years ago. The following is quoted as the first verse :

> Ben he was a coachman rare
> (' Jarvey ! Jarvey ! ' ' Here I am, yer honour '),
> Crikey ! how he used to swear !
> How he'd swear, and how he'd drive,
> Number two hundred and sixty-five.
> Tamaroo ! Tamaroo ! Tamaroo !

Dr. Sweeting, the present music-master at Winchester, says, ' The song " Tamaroo " is quite unknown here now, and if it was sung here seventy or eighty years ago, I should imagine that that was only because it was generally well known.   Dickens' allusion to it seems to suggest that it was a song he had heard, and he utilized its character to label one of his characters in his own fanciful way.'

TARRY TROUSERS (*D. & S.* 39)

An old folk-song.   A mother wants her daughter to marry a tailor, and not wait for her sailor bold, telling her that it is quite time she was a bride.   The daughter says :

> My mother wants me to wed with a tailor,
> And not give me my heart's delight,
> But give me the man with the tarry trousers,
> That shine to me like diamonds bright.

TELL ME, SHEPHERDS (*E.D.* 2)   *Mazzinghi.*

Glee.   ' Ye Shepherds, tell me ' (or ' The Wreath ');

THE BRAVE OLD OAK (*S.B.S.* 2.)

Words by *H. F. Chorley.*   *E. J. Loder.*

> A song for the oak, the brave old oak,
> Who hath ruled in the greenwood long ;
> Here's health and renown to his broad green crown,
> And his fifty arms so strong !

THE BULL IN THE CHINA SHOP

See p. 111.

THE CHERUB THAT SITS UP ALOFT (*U.T.* 5)

From ' Poor Jack.'   *C. Dibdin.*

> For d'ye see, there's a cherub sits smiling aloft
> To keep watch for the life of Poor Jack.

> (*Last two lines of verse* 3.)

THE CORDIAL THAT SPARKLED FOR HELEN (*O.C.S.* 61)

Moore's *Irish Melodies.*

THE DASHING WHITE SERGEANT (*D.C.* 28)

Words by *General Burgoyne.*   *H. R. Bishop.*

> If I had a beau, for a soldier who'd go,
> Do you think I'd say no? No, no, not I.

THE GAY, THE GAY AND FESTIVE SEASON (*O.M.F.*)

See ' The Light Guitar.'

THE GREAT SEA SNAKE

Set to the air ' Rampant Moll.'

> Perhaps you have all of you heard of a yarn
> Of a famous large sea snake,
> That once was seen off the Isle Pitcairn
> And caught by Admiral Blake.

See p. 16.

THE IVY GREEN (*P.P.* 6.)

Words by *Dickens.* The most popular musical setting is that by *Henry Russell.*

THE LIGHT GUITAR (*S.B.T.* 1, *O.C.S.*)

Barnett.

> Oh leave the gay and festive scene,
>   The halls of dazzling light,
> And rove with me through forests green
>   Beneath the silent night.

THE MILLER OF THE DEE (*O.M.F.* ii. 1)

Words, c. 1762.   Tune, 1728.

Referring to a disused boiler and a great iron wheel,
Dickens says they are

> Like the Miller of questionable jollity in the song.
> They cared for Nobody, no not they, and Nobody
> cared for them.

The air is found in *The Quaker's Opera*, 1728.

THE RATCATCHER'S DAUGHTER (*Out of Season*)

See p. 98.

THE SEVEN AGES (*S.B.S.* 14)

See pp. 91, 92.

THE SOLDIER, TIRED (*S.B.C.* 4)   *Arne.*

Dr. Arne translated the words from the *Artaserse* of
Metastasio. This song was the great ' show song ' for
sopranos for many years. It was originally sung by
Miss Brent.

> The soldier, tired of war's alarms,
> Forswears the clang of hostile arms,
>   And scorns the spear and shield ;
> But if the brazen trumpet sound,
> He burns with conquest to be crowned,
>   And dares again the field.

THE WOODPECKER TAPPING (*D.C.* 36, *L.D.* 35, *S.B.T.* 1, *M.C.* 25)

Words by *Moore*.   *M. Kelly.*

Every leaf was at rest, and I heard not a sound
But the woodpecker tapping the hollow beech-tree.

THE YOUNG MAY MOON

See p. 131.

THEN FAREWELL, MY TRIM-BUILT WHERRY (*O.M.F.*)

See p. 133.

THERE LET 'EM BE, MERRY AND FREE, TOOR-RUL-LAL-LA (*O.C.S.* 56)

Probably original.

THOUGH LOST TO SIGHT, TO MEMORY DEAR (*D. & S.* 48)

Words and music by *G. Linley*.

Tho' lost to sight, to mem'ry dear
Thou ever wilt remain,
One only hope my heart can cheer :
The hope to meet again.

THROWN ON THE WIDE WORLD (*O.M.F.*)

See p. 133.

TIME OF DAY (*S.B.C.* 8)

See p. 92.

'TIS THE VOICE OF THE SLUGGARD (*M.C.* 9)   *Dr. Watts.*

'TWAS EVER THUS FROM CHILDHOOD'S HOUR (*O.C.S.* 56, *D.C.* 38) (' Oh ever,' &c.)

Words by *Moore*.

From ' Lalla Rookh.' Has been set to music by S. Glover, E. Souper, and Verini.

VILLIKENS AND HIS DINAH

> Sung by Mr. Robson and by S. Cowell.

> Composer unknown.   A very popular song 1850–1860.

>> It's of a liquor merchant who in London did dwell,
>> He had but one darter, a beautiful gal.
>> Her name it was Dinah, just sixteen years old,
>> And she had a large fortune in silver and gold.
>> To my too-ral-lal loo-ral-li loo-ral-li-day.

WAPPING OLD STAIRS (*U.T* 3)   *J. Percy.*

WEEP FOR THE HOUR (*O.M.F.*)

> See p. 133.

WE MET (*O.C.S.* 36, *S.B.T.* 11)   *T. H. Bayly.*

> The story of a girl who was compelled by her mother
> to jilt her true love and marry some one else.   The story
> ends with the words misquoted by Swiveller :

>> The world may think me gay,
>> For my feelings I smother—
>> Oh ! *thou* hast been the cause
>> Of this anguish, my mother !

WE'RE A'NODDIN' (*B.H.* 39)

> *Anonymous.*

> A once popular Scotch song.

>> O we're a' noddin, nid nid noddin,
>> O we're a' noddin at our house at home ;
>> How's o' wi' ye, kimmer ?   And how do ye thrive,
>> And how many bairns hae ye now ?   Bairns I hae five.

WE WON'T GO HOME TILL MORNING (*P.P.* 7)

> Said in the *London Singer's Magazine* (c. 1839) to be
> written and composed by C. Blondel (' adapted and ar-
> ranged ' might be more correct).   The tune is founded

on an air known as Malbrough, or Malbrook, which originated during the Duke of Marlborough's campaign, 1704-1709, known as 'The War of the Spanish Succession.'

WHAT ARE THE WILD WAVES SAYING ?

Words by *J. E. Carpenter*.   *Stephen Glover*.

This duet was founded upon the question little Paul Dombey asks his sister :

> I want to know what it says—the sea, Floy, what is it that it keeps on saying ?

WHEN HE WHO ADORES THEE (*O.C.S.* 35)

Words by *Moore*.

In *Irish Melodies* to the air ' The Fox's Sleep.'

WHEN I WENT TO LUNNON TOWN, SIRS (*G.E.* 15)

Probably original.   The nearest I have found to it is—

THE ASTONISHED COUNTRYMAN, OR, A BUSTLING PICTURE OF LONDON.

> When first I came to London Town,
>   How great was my surprise,
> Thought I, the world's turned upside down,
>   Such wonders met my eyes.

And in *The Universal Songster*—

> When I arrived in London Town,
> I got my lesson pat, &c.

WHEN IN DEATH I SHALL CALM RECLINE

Moore's *Irish Melodies*.

In 1833 Dickens wrote a travesty called *O' Thello*, in which is a humorous solo of eight lines, to be sung to the air to which the above is set.

WHEN LOVELY WOMAN STOOPS TO FOLLY (*O.C.S.* 56)

' Do my pretty Olivia,' cried she, ' let us have that
little melancholy air your papa was so fond of ; your
sister Sophy has already obliged us. Do, child, it will
please your old father.' She complied in a manner
so exquisitely pathetic, as moved me.

> When lovely woman stoops to folly,
>   And finds, too late, that men betray,
> What charm can soothe her melancholy ?
>   What art can wash her guilt away ?

(Goldsmith's *Vicar of Wakefield,* ch. xxiv.)

WHEN THE HEART OF A MAN (*D.C.* 24, *O.M.F.* iii. 14)

Words by *Gay* (*Beggar's Opera*). Set to a seventeenth-
century air.

> If the heart of a man is depressed with care,
> The mist is dispelled when a woman appears,
> Like the notes of a fiddle she sweetly, sweetly
> Raises our spirits and charms our ears.

WHEN THE STORMY WINDS (*D.C.* 21, *D. & S.* 23)

Words by *Campbell,* who may have taken them
from an earlier source. See ' You Gentlemen of
England.'

WHITE SAND (*L.D.* i. 32)

An old glee. See p. 106.

WHO PASSES BY THIS ROAD SO LATE (*L.D.* i. 1)

(Blandois' Song.)

Words by *C. Dickens.*   *H. R. S. Dalton.*

An old French children's singing game. Dickens' words
are a literal translation. See *Eighty Singing Games*
(Kidson and Moffat).

WHO RAN TO CATCH ME WHEN I FELL (*O.C.S.* 38)

From Ann Taylor's nursery song ' My Mother.'

WIFE SHALL DANCE AND I WILL SING, SO MERRILY PASS THE DAY

From ' Begone, dull care ' (q.v.).

WILL WATCH, THE BOLD SMUGGLER (*Out of Season*)

John Davy.

YANKEE DOODLE (*U.T., A.N.*)

Mr. F. Kidson has traced this to ' A selection of Scotch, English, Irish, and Foreign Airs,' published in Glasgow by James Aird, c. 1775 or 1776.

YET LOV'D I AS MAN NE'ER LOVED (*O.C.S.* 50)

Words by *William Mee.*   *Millard.*

From ' Alice Gray.'

> She's all my fancy painted her,
>   She's lovely, she's divine,
> But her heart it is another's,
>   It never can be mine.
> Yet lov'd I as ne'er man loved,
>   A love without decay,
> Oh my heart, my heart is breaking,
>   For the love of *Alice Gray* !

' Alice Gray.' A ballad, sung by Miss Stephens, Miss Palon, and Miss Grant. Composed and inscribed to Mr. A. Pettet by Mrs. Philip Millard.

Published by A. Pettet, Hanway Street.

YOU GENTLEMEN OF ENGLAND (*D. & S.* 23)

Old English Ballad.

A seventeenth-century song, the last line of each verse being ' When the stormy winds do blow.'

Young Love Lived Once (*S.B.S.* 20)

In *Sketches by Boz* this sentence occurs :

> 'When we say a " shed " we do not mean the con-
> servatory kind of building which, according to the old
> song, Love frequented when a young man.'

The song referred to is by T. Moore.

> Young love lived once in a humble shed,
> Where roses breathing,
> And woodbines wreathing,
> Around the lattice their tendrils spread,
> As wild and sweet as the life he led.

It is one of the songs in *M.P., or The Blue-Stocking*,
a comic opera in three acts.

M

INDEX OF MUSICAL INSTRUMENTS

INDEX OF CHARACTERS

GENERAL INDEX

A LIST OF VOCAL AND INSTRUMENTAL MUSIC

ASSOCIATED WITH DICKENS AND WITH THE CHARACTERS IN HIS NOVELS

All these pieces are in the possession of Mr. W. Miller, Librarian of the Dickens Fellowship

Songs in the VILLAGE COQUETTES. Words by *Charles Dickens*. Music by *Hullah*.

THE IVY GREEN. Song. Words by *Charles Dickens*. Music by *Mrs. Henry Dale*.

THE IVY GREEN. Song. Music by *A. De Belfer*.

THE IVY GREEN. Song. Music by *W. Lovell Phillips*.

THE IVY GREEN. Song. Music by *Henry Russell*.

  (This song has been published by almost every music publisher in London and America.)

Introduction and familiar variations on THE IVY GREEN arranged for the pianoforte by *Ricardo Linter*.

Russell's Song THE IVY GREEN, with introduction and variations for the pianoforte by *Stephen Glover*.

THE IVY GREEN as a vocal duet. Music by *Henry Russell*.

A CHRISTMAS CAROL. Words by *Charles Dickens*. Music by *Henry Russell*.

A CHRISTMAS CAROL. Words by *Charles Dickens*. Music by *Henry Russell* to the tune of OLD KING COLE.

BOLD TURPIN. Words by *Charles Dickens*. Music by *Sir J. F. Bridge*.

PICKWICK. Set to Music by *George L. Jeune*. Words by *George Soane*.

THE WERY LAST OBSERVATIONS OF WELLER SENIOR TO BOZ ON HIS DEPARTURE FROM LONDON. Written and sung by *J. M. Field, Esq.* Adapted to an old air. Boston, 1842.

THE ORIGINAL SET OF PICKWICK QUADRILLES. Edited by ' *Boz* ' *Junior*.

SAM WELLER'S ADVENTURES. Reprinted in *The Life and Times of James Catnach*.

GABRIEL GRUB. Cantata Seria Buffa. Adapted by *Frederick Wood*. Music by *George Fox*.

PICKWICK TARANTELLE.

MR. STIGGINS. Song. Maliciously written and composed by ' *Tony Weller*.'

THE PICKWICK QUADRILLE. Composed by *Fred Revallin*.

THE PICKWICK LANCERS. Composed by *Camille D'Aubert*.

PICKWICK. Songs and Dances by *Edward Solomon*. Words of songs by *Sir F. C. Burnand*.

OLIVER TWIST. Written by *H. Copeland* from a song by *W. T. Townsend*.

THE ARTFUL DODGER. Written by *Charles Sloman* and *Sam Cowell*. Music by *Fred Bridgeman*. Sung by *Sam Cowell*.

NICHOLAS NICKLEBY QUADRILLE AND NICKLEBY GALOP. By *Sydney Vernon*.

MASTER HUMPHREY'S CLOCK, 'DID YOU HEAR ANYTHING KNOCK?' Song by *Beuler*.

MASTER HUMPHREY'S QUADRILLES. Music by ' *Boz* ' *Junior*.

THE CHIMES OF MASTER HUMPHREY'S CLOCK. Arranged for the pianoforte by *Charles Arnold*.

THE GHOST OF THE BARON OF GROG-SWIG. Written by *John Major*. Arranged by *J. Monro*.

LITTLE NELL. Words by *Miss Charlotte Young*. Music by *George Linley*.

LITTLE NELL. Composed by *George Linley*. Arranged for the pianoforte by *Carlo Totti*.

NELL. Song. Composed by *H. L. Winter*.

LITTLE NELL. By *Miss Hawley*.

LITTLE NELL. Waltz by *Dan Godfrey*.

NELL. Words by *Edward Oxenford*. Music by *Alfred J. Caldicott*.

LITTLE NELLIE'S POLKA. Composed by *J. Pridham*.

BARNABY RUDGE TARANTELLE. By *Clementine Ward*.

DOLLY VARDEN. Ballad. Words and Music by *Cotsford Dick*.

G. W. *Hunt's* Popular Song DOLLY VARDEN.

DOLLY VARDEN. Comic Song. Words by *Frank W. Green*. Music by *Alfred Lee*.

Vance's DOLLY VARDEN. Written, composed, and sung by *Alfred G. Vance.*

G. W. Moore's Great Song DRESSED AS A DOLLY VARDEN. Written, composed, and sung by *G. W. Moore.*

DOLLY VARDEN'S WEDDING. Comic Song. Written, composed, and arranged by *T. R. Tebley.*

DOLLY VARDEN WALTZ. By *Henry Parker.*

DOLLY VARDEN VALSE. Composed by *Sara Leumas.*

THE DOLLY VARDEN POLKA. By *Brinley Richards.*

THE DOLLY VARDEN POLKA. By *W. C. Levey.*

DOLLY VARDEN POLKA. By *Henry Parker.*

THE DOLLY VARDEN POLKA. Arranged by *T. C. Lewis.* Composed by *G. Discongi.*

DOLLY VARDEN POLKA. By *George Gough.*

DOLLY VARDEN GALOP. By *Charles Coote, jun.*

DOLLY VARDEN SCHOTTISCHE. By *Helene.*

THE DOLLY VARDEN SCHOTTISCHE. By *H. King.*

DOLLY VARDEN GAVOTTE. By *Clementine Ward.*

DOLLY VARDEN QUADRILLE. By *Henry Parker.*

DOLLY VARDEN QUADRILLE, on old English Tunes. By *C. H. R. Marriott.*

MAYPOLE HUGH. Song. Words by *Charles Bradberry.* Music by *George Fox.*

YANKEE NOTES FOR ENGLISH CIRCULATION ; or BOZ IN A-MERRY-KEY. Comic Song. Written by *James Briton.* Music arranged to an American Air by *Geo. Loder.*

THE CHRISTMAS CAROL QUADRILLES. By *Edwin Merriott.*

TINY TIM. Words by *Edward Oxenford.* Music by *Alfred J. Caldicott.*

TINY TIM. Words by *Harry Lynn.* Music by *W. Knowles.*

THE SONG OF CHRISTMAS. Song sung in *A Christmas Carol* at the Theatre Royal, Adelphi. Composed by *C. Herbert Rodwell.*

TINY TIM. Written and composed by *Arthur Wingham.*

' GOD BLESS US EVERY ONE.' Words by *Geo. Cooper.* Music by *Herbert Foster.*

THE CHIMES. Song. Written by *J. E. Carpenter.* Music composed by *F. Nicholls Crouch.*

THE CHIMES. By *Jullien.*

THE CHIMES QUADRILLES. By *Henry Oakey*.

THE CHIMES QUADRILLES. By *Lancelott*.

THE CHIMES GAVOTTE. For the pianoforte, with bell accompaniment (ad lib.). Composed by *Wm. West*, Organist and Choirmaster of St. Margaret Pattens (Rood Lane, E.C.).

LILLIAN. Ballad from *The Chimes*. The Poetry by *Fanny E. Lacey*. Music by *Edward L. Hime*.

THE SPIRIT OF THE CHIMES. Written and composed by *Fanny E. Lacey*.

THE CRICKET ON THE HEARTH. Song. By *James E. Stewart*, Cincinnati, U.S.A.

THE CRICKET ON THE HEARTH. A Domestic Ballad. Written by *Edward J. Gill*. Music by *J. Blewitt*.

THE CRICKET POLKA.

THE CRICKET POLKA. Composed by *Jullien*.

THE CRICKET ON THE HEARTH QUADRILLES. Composed by *S. D. Saunders*.

THE CRICKET ON THE HEARTH. A set of Quadrilles. By *T. L. Rowbotham*.

THE CRICKET ON THE HEARTH. A new Christmas Quadrille. By *F. Lancelott*.

THE NEW CRICKET POLKA. Composed by *Johann Lupeski*.

THE BATTLE OF LIFE. Song. Words by *O. C. Lynn*. Music by *R. Graylott*. Published in *The Illustrated London News*, March 20, 1847

THE FRUIT GATHERERS' SONG (' The Battle of Life '). Written by *Fanny E. Lacey*. Composed by *Edwin Flood*.

THE HAUNTED MAN QUADRILLES. By *Wm. West*.

WHAT ARE THE WILD WAVES SAYING? Written by *J. E. Carpenter*. Music by *Stephen Glover*.

WHAT ARE THE WILD WAVES SAYING? (*Stephen Glover*). Arranged for the pianoforte by *Brinley Richards*.

A VOICE FROM THE WAVES (an answer to the above). Words by *R. Ryan*. Music by *Stephen Glover*.

LITTLE PAUL BALLAD. Poetry by *Miss C. Young*. Music by *W. T. Wrighton*.

PAUL. Song. Words by *Edward Oxenford*. Music by *Alfred J. Caldicott*.

FLORENCE. Song. Written by *Charles Jeffrey*

POOR FLORENCE. Song. Music composed by *W. T. Wrighton.*

WALTER AND FLORENCE. Song. Written by *Johanna Chandler.*
Music by *Stephen Glover.*

DOMBEY AND SON QUADRILLE. By *Miss Harriet Frances
Brown.*

THE DAVID COPPERFIELD POLKA. Composed by *W. Wilson.*

THE MICAWBER QUADRILLE (played in the drama of *Little
Em'ly,* at the Olympic Theatre, in 1869). Composed by *J.
Winterbottom.*

LITTLE EM'LY VALSES. By *John Winterbottom.* (Played in
the drama of *Little Em'ly,* at the Olympic Theatre,
in 1869.)

THE LITTLE EM'LY POLKA. Composed by *W. G. Severn.*

AGNES ; or I HAVE LOVED YOU ALL MY LIFE. Ballad. Written
by *Ger Vere Irving.* Composed by *Gerald Stanley.*

DORA ; or THE CHILD-WIFE'S FAREWELL. Ballad. Written by
George Linley. Composed by *Gerald Stanley.*

PEGGOTTY THE WANDERER. Ballad. Written by *William
Martin.* Music by *James William Etherington.*

DORA TO AGNES. Song. Words by *Charles Jeffrey.* Music by
J. H. Tully.

LITTLE BLOSSOM. Ballad by *Stephen Glover.* Words by
Charlotte Young.

HOUSEHOLD WORDS. Duet. Written by *Charlotte Young.*
Composed by *John Blockley.*

Songs and Ballads from *Bleak House* :

> (1) THE SONG OF ESTHER SUMMERSON, ' Farewell to the
> Old Home.' Written by *Charles Jeffrey.* Music by
> *Charles W. Glover.*

> (2) ADA CLARE. Written by *Charles Jeffrey.* Set to
> Music by *Charles W. Glover.*

POOR JO ! Ballad. Written by *H. B. Farnie.* Composed by
C. F. R. Marriott.

POOR JO ! Song and Chorus. Written by *W. R. Gordon.* Composed by *Alfred Lee.*

' JO.' Galop for the pianoforte upon airs from the celebrated
drama, by *Edward Solomon.*

' HE WAS WERY GOOD TO ME.' Poor Jo's song. Written and
composed by *Alfred Allen.*

THE TOKEN FLOWERS. Song founded on ' Cadby's Flowers ' in *Bleak House*. Written by *Joseph Edward Carpenter*. Music by *B. Moligne*.

HARD TIMES. Polka. By *C. W.*

LITTLE DORRIT. Ballad. Written and composed by *John Caulfield*.

LITTLE DORRIT. Song. Written by *Henry Abrahams*. Music by *C. Stanley*.

LITTLE DORRIT'S POLKA. Composed by *Jules Norman*.

AS YOU LIKE IT ; or LITTLE DORRIT'S POLKA. By *W. H. Montgomery*.

LITTLE DORRIT'S VIGIL. By the composer of LITTLE NELL.

LITTLE DORRIT'S SCHOTTISCHE. Composed by *W. M. Parker*.

LITTLE DORRIT SERENADE. By *Clementine Ward*.

' MY DEAR OLD HOME.' Ballad. Written by *J. E. Carpenter*. Composed by *John Blockley*.

WHO PASSES BY THIS ROAD SO LATE ? Blandois' song from *Little Dorrit*. Words by *Charles Dickens*. Music by *H. R. S. Dalton*. (This song was suggested to Dickens by the French song entitled ' Le Chevalier du guet.')

FLOATING AWAY BALLAD. Written by *J. E. Carpenter*. Music by *John Blockley*.

ALL THE YEAR ROUND ; or THE SEARCH FOR HAPPINESS. Song. Written by *W. S. Passmore*. Composed by *John Blockley*.

ALL THE YEAR ROUND QUADRILLES. By *E. Frewin*.

ALL THE YEAR ROUND VARSOVIANA. By *W. H. Montgomery*.

THE TWO CITIES QUADRILLES. By *W. H. Montgomery*.

TOM TIDDLER'S POLKA. Composed by *W. Wilson*.

GREAT EXPECTATIONS. Ballad.

Coote's Lancers, ' SOMEBODY'S LUGGAGE.'

MRS. LIRRIPER'S QUADRILLE. Written by *Adrian Victor*.

JENNY WREN (THE DOLL'S DRESSMAKER). Song. Words by *Edward Oxenford*. Music by *Alfred J. Caldicott*.

JENNY WREN QUADRILLES. Arranged by *Rosabel*.

MUGBY JUNCTION GALOP. By *Charles Coote, jun.*

NO THOROUGHFARE GALOP. Composed by *Charles Coote, jun.*